Counseling Tips for Elementary School Principals

Counseling
Tips for
Elementary
School
Principals

Jeffrey A. Kottler
Elaine K. McEwan

CORWIN PRESS, INC.
A Sage Publications Company
Thousand Oaks, California

For information:

Corwin Press, Inc.
A Sage Publications Company
2455 Teller Road
Thousand Oaks, California 91320
E-mail: order@corwinpress.com

SAGE Publications Ltd.
6 Bonhill Street
London EC2A 4PU
United Kingdom

SAGE Publications India Pvt. Ltd.
M-32 Market
Greater Kailash I
New Delhi 110 048 India

Printed in the United States of America

Library of Congress Cataloging-in-Publication Data

Kottler, Jeffrey A.
    Counseling tips for elementary school principals / Jeffrey A. Kottler, Elaine K. McEwan
        p.   cm.
    ISBN 0-8039-6722-5 (cloth: acid-free paper)
    ISBN 0-8039-6723-3 (pbk.: acid-free paper)
    1. Counseling in elementary education—United States. 2. Elementary school principals—United States. 3. Interpersonal relations—United States.   I. McEwan, Elaine K., 1941– II. Title.
    LB1027.5 .K664 1998
    372.14—ddc21   98-25538

This book is printed on acid-free paper.

99 00 01 02 03 04 05 10 9 8 7 6 5 4 3 2 1

Production Editor: S. Marlene Head
Editorial Assistant: Kristen L. Gibson
Typesetter: Rebecca Evans
Cover Designer: Michelle Lee

Contents

————————

Preface

A fter a typical action-packed day helping students, teachers, and parents, many a school principal has quietly wondered whether the time spent earning a degree in administration might better have been spent in taking certification in counseling. Although counseling responsibilities may not appear in your formal job description, one of the critical steps to becoming an effective instructional leader is the development and maintenance of positive relationships with students, staff, and parents.

How does a principal go about keeping the cogs and gears of positive interaction and interpersonal relationships well oiled and smoothly turning? By doing things like serving as an advocate for students and talking with them regularly regarding aspects of their school life; by encouraging open communication among staff members; by demonstrating concern and openness in the consideration of student, teacher, and/or parental problems and participating in the resolution of such problems where appropriate; by modeling appropriate human relations skills; by developing and maintaining high morale; and by systematically collecting and responding to student, staff, and parent concerns. This is indeed a tall order for the majority of us, especially when you consider the obstacles in our way.

Achieving high marks in the "human" arena of effective instructional leadership is made especially challenging by three realities: (a) the diverse pressures and problems of contemporary society that manifest themselves in our students, staff, and parents; (b) inadequate administrative preparation to prepare us for the variety, severity, constancy, and complexity of the problems; and (c) our own personal "emotional" baggage that often clouds our ability to remain objective and control our impulses.

Consider what you could (and often do) face on an average Monday morning:

- Secretaries in a panic over some new mandate by the school board
- A stack of messages left on the answering machine over the weekend, many of which involve parental complaints and threats
- An assortment of student disciplinary matters requiring some intervention
- A half dozen memos from the district central office, most of which neither make sense nor seem particularly useful
- An inquiry from the media wanting an interview about perceived low performance in school achievement
- Several different teachers who need reassurance, approval, or some time to talk about a personal issue

Your administrative training program (even if it is recent) likely contained little to prepare you for the daily realities of life in the average school. You no doubt took courses in administrative theory, finance, school-community relations, and school law. But you'll find precious little in those syllabi to guide you in how to deal with recalcitrant students, flighty staff members, or protesting parents. Your lack of training and expertise will not suffice to keep the problems at bay, however. But your deficits in this area will almost surely reduce your effectiveness in affecting student achievement, teacher morale, and parental support.

Don't take our word for it that counseling and consulting skills are crucial to a principal's success. In focus groups conducted by the publisher with elementary principals, these school administrators were asked to identify the area in which they most needed additional training. In other words: Which book would you most like to consult with that you don't have as part of your personal library? This book was born because the participants overwhelmingly identified counseling and communication skills as a primary area of need.

The intent of this book is not to equip you with the background or the skills to function in the role of counselor or human relations consultant—that is what school counselors, psychologists, and social workers do. The reality of daily school life, however, is that you must serve in helping roles daily. As you spend time in classrooms conducting teacher observations, you cannot help but notice the children who seem tired, troubled, or disengaged. As you spend time on the school playground or attend athletic events on weekends, you will chat with children who trust you, children who want someone to listen to them and understand them. As you speak with parents and staff members about the students in your school, you will be required to demonstrate a high degree of interpersonal sensitivity and skill. It is our hope, therefore, that this book will introduce you to the basic methodology of counseling and consulting just as its predecessor, *Teacher as Counselor*, did for teachers.

Although we cannot make a counselor out of you in seven simple steps (years of supervised practice are needed), we certainly can sensitize you to the basic ideas and skills that are involved in being a helper.

Who This Book Is For

This book is intended for two audiences. First, it can be used as a resource text or supplementary reading in a training program (either formal or informal) for aspiring or beginning principals. Many districts see the need to augment the traditional university administrative training program, and this book will provide helpful information not available in most certification programs. Among the highest priorities is to ensure that newly hired principals are equipped with professional and personal survival skills that are likely to increase their probability of success. Acquiring counseling and consulting skills is an important learning task for beginning principals who are endeavoring to earn the trust and respect of their students, staff, and parent/community.

The second audience is the current population of principals who are looking for ways to improve their counseling and consulting skills. Experienced administrators know they must constantly hone their human relations ability if they are to improve student achievement, empower teachers, and gain parental support.

A Note to Readers

The subjects discussed in this book do not lend themselves to learning by passive means. Although reading chapters about helping skills will enable you to conceptualize how and why various counseling strategies are applied, there is no way these complex behaviors can become part of your own interpersonal style without considerable practice. This personal integration can take two basic forms:

1. After each idea is presented, ask yourself how you can make it part of your life, how you could use the techniques to enrich your relationships at work and home.
2. Find opportunities to practice new skills in enough situations so that they will become a natural part of your interpersonal style.

At the end of each chapter we have included a list of suggested readings should you want to learn more about a particular subject. Of even more importance, we have provided a number of activities that you might complete if you want to apply what you learn to real-life situations. This kind of practice is, of course, one of the most important concepts of effective education: If we expect to influence the way our students, parents, and staff think, feel, and act, we must develop structures in which they can apply what they learn in multiple situations. It certainly applies to your own attempts to master a set of very difficult skills in a very short period of time.

Overview of the Contents

Chapter 1 introduces you to the multiple roles the principal plays in counseling and consulting with students, staff, and parents. You'll meet some current principals who are wrestling with the same issues that you confront in a typical week.

Chapter 2 describes how you can assess more systematically a variety of concerns and problems (some easily solved and many more too complex for pat solutions) that you might encounter in students, staff, and parents. Understanding the symptoms of conditions like depression, anxiety, attention deficit hyperactivity disorder, substance abuse, and conduct disorders will help you know when it's time to call in other experts to assist in diagnosis and treatment.

Chapter 3 provides a quick overview of the counseling process as it operates in brief, influential interactions. Principals end up doing quite a lot of "instant counseling" with their staff, parents, and students. Unfortunately, such efforts aren't as helpful as they could be if you felt better prepared to handle the problems as they arise.

Specific helping skills and examples of how to use each skill with students, staff, and parents are provided in Chapter 4, and Chapter 5 will help you transfer your counseling skills to working with small groups. Shared decision making and problem solving will empower students, staff, and parents alike. But first, you need to know when to use small groups and how to best lead and facilitate them.

Chapter 6 focuses on dealing with parents who are angry, troubled, fearful, and even hostile. You'll find ways to improve your parent-student conferences, how to regroup when Plan A doesn't work, and how to keep your own emotions under control when under attack.

Finally, Chapter 7 discusses counseling skills specific to the teacher-principal relationship. Issues like counseling the ineffective teacher, dealing with legal questions, and how to handle close friendships with staff members are just a few of the questions to which you'll find answers.

We hope that after reading *Counseling Tips for Elementary School Principals* you'll be encouraged to devote the time and energy needed to expand and refine your helping skills. In the current climate of accountability, you may be tempted to underestimate the power of positive human relations and the importance of a mentally healthy school environment when it comes to the bottom line (i.e., test scores). Personal experience has shown us, and research bears it out, that student achievement is higher in schools where principals are perceived as strong instructional leaders. In environments where students feel affirmed and respected, they will be more motivated to learn and achieve. When teachers are empowered and their voices are heard, they will transmit their confidence and sense of efficacy to students. Finally, when parents are understood and appreciated, they will join with us in solving the problems that almost every family faces at one time or another. You are the person who can make this happen.

JEFFREY A. KOTTLER
Las Vegas, Nevada
ELAINE K. MCEWAN
Tucson, Arizona

About the Authors

Jeffrey A. Kottler has worked as a teacher, counselor, professor, and administrator in a variety of educational settings. He is a prolific author of more than 30 books written for teachers, counselors, therapists, and the public. Several of his other Corwin titles include *On Being a Teacher* (1993), *Teacher as Counselor* (1993), *Classrooms Under the Influence: Addicted Families/Addicted Students* (1995), *What's Really Said in the Teachers' Lounge: Provocative Ideas About Cultures and Classrooms* (1997), *Success With Challenging Students* (1997), and *Secrets for Secondary School Teachers: How to Succeed in Your First Year* (1998).

Elaine K. McEwan is a partner in the McEwan-Adkins Group, an educational consulting firm. She received her Ed.D. in educational administration from Northern Illinois University. She has been a teacher, librarian, elementary school principal, and assistant superintendent for instruction. McEwan is the author of more than two dozen books for parents, children, and educators, including *Attention Deficit Disorder* (1996), *Nobody Likes Me: What to Do When Your Child Can't Make Friends* (1996), *When Kids Say No to School: Helping Students-at-Risk* (1998), *The Principal's Guide to Attention Deficit Hyperactivity Disorder* (1998), and *How to Deal With Parents Who Are Angry, Troubled, Afraid, or Just Plain Crazy* (1998).

1

The Multiple Hats
of School Principals

Quick! What came to your mind when you first imagined being a school principal? You probably envisioned strolling through the quiet hallways of a well-appointed school where—much like the mythical Lake Wobegon—all the children were above average, all the teachers were well adjusted and effective, and every mom and dad was a paragon of parenting virtue. Unfortunately, this mythical school existed only until the ink dried on your contract. Instead of paradise you found a school teeming with interpersonal crises, conflict, problems, issues, anger, and fear.

For principals of an earlier era, their competence was judged primarily on their skill as organizers and managers. Indeed, developing schedules, ordering and unpacking materials, and making sure that buses ran on time were considered to be the chief tasks of the school principal. The job description has expanded exponentially, however. Buses, books, and business are, of course, still important. By no means, however, are these the standard by which our students, staff, and parents rate our effectiveness. They will judge us by who we are and how we interact with others.

The Principal's Mission

When you reminisce about your own educational experiences and reflect on those educators who were most inspirational, who made the greatest difference in your life, we suspect that you recall things more intangible than their well-honed teaching or administrative

1

skills. There was something about their personal qualities, the ways they carried themselves, their integrity and honesty, that earned your respect and trust. It was not just the knowledge they held that made them such wonderful educators, it was the personal and passionate way in which they communicated their caring for you and others.

Assuming this phenomenon is fairly universal—in other words, that all of the constituencies with whom you interact are influenced not only by your technical expertise but also by your sense of caring, competence, and compassion—then principals really must have specialized training in all their various roles. You have had systematic education in how to structure a school referendum, in how to read a school budget, and in how to examine the legalities of a due process hearing. But what about training in the other roles you will play in people's lives—as a model of personal effectiveness, as a compassionate listener, as a skilled helper?

You are called on daily, if not hourly, to wear a number of different hats and to function in a variety of diverse roles for which you may not be adequately prepared. How do you handle things when a parent bursts into your office demanding that a teacher be fired? How do you deal with the student who refuses to follow the rules in his classroom and offers teacher harassment and abuse as his excuse? What do you do when you suspect that a child is abusing drugs or is suffering from an eating disorder? What do you say to the teacher who shares a heretofore unknown problem from her past? How do you act when a student solicits your promise to keep a secret, but then tells you that she is breaking the law and intends to continue doing so? How do you handle a breakdown in communication between an instructional team leader and his fellow teachers?

By virtue of choosing education as a profession, you have dedicated yourself first to influencing children's lives. You probably sought an administrative position to widen your scope of influence to also include teachers and parents, realizing that education is a team effort. To accomplish this mission you do so much more than merely manage and administer your school. Where you make the most difference is in the relationships you develop with children, staff, and parents that are built on trust, mutual respect, and true affection. When these alliances are sound and healthy, individuals will come to you with their problems and openly share of themselves. But more often, they cry out for help in subtle ways via signs that you will not be able to read without additional training.

Your mission, should you choose to accept it, is to develop yourself as a skilled helper, a task that will involve mastering a number of counseling and consulting skills. This training will enhance your ability to observe and make sense of what others, both children and adults, are thinking, feeling, and doing. It will allow you to gain meaningful access into their inner worlds, to earn their trust, and to truly understand what they are experiencing. From such an empathic position you can help them feel understood. You can help them reach greater clarity. You can help them make difficult decisions. When indicated, you should urge them to seek professional help. And they will listen to you because you have credible helping skills and an authentic interest in their welfare.

Counseling Skills for Principals

Whether you like it or not, whether you're prepared for the role or not, you will be sought out as a confidant of students, teachers, and parents who have nowhere else to turn. They will expect a number of things from you, some that you cannot deliver (finding the "right" answer) and some that you should not deliver (taking over their lives and telling them what to do). Nevertheless, if you are equipped with some counseling skills, basic helping strategies like listening and responding, you will be amazed at the services you can render in helping individuals gain enhanced clarity of their feelings, better understanding of their motives, and greater resolve in following through on a plan to change their behavior. Adding counseling skills to your repertoire of educational methodologies will help you in several important ways:

1. *You will notice an improvement in your personal relationships.* Because learning counseling skills will increase your sensitivity and responsiveness, this training will affect the ways you relate to other people. You will notice yourself becoming more attuned to others' feelings. You will become more clear in your communications and more expressive of your own needs. Finally, you will experience a renewed commitment to work toward greater intimacy in your relationships with friends and family.

2. *You will become more respected as a leader in your school.* Just as high-level interpersonal skills allow you to create better relationships in your personal life, they can also give you the confidence and ability to forge constructive alliances with fellow administrators, your staff members, parents, and children. Everyone wants a friend who listens well, who is empathic, who is a clear thinker, and who responds to one's needs. One other benefit: When you learn to speak the language of counselors, you will be able to make more appropriate referrals for individuals whose problems are at the crisis point.

3. *You will become more influential in every aspect of school life.* Those with whom you interact on a daily basis will respect you and respond to you not only for your educational expertise but also for your caring and compassion. Counseling skills will, quite simply, allow you to create better relationships with everyone in a shorter period of time. Students will be more inclined to trust you and to work hard to gain your respect if they sense the same from you. Staff members will be more willing to go the extra mile and become team players when they perceive your desire to listen to their concerns. Parents will be more supportive if they experience the ability on your part to understand their needs and frustrations. These skills can thus form the glue, bonding together everything else you have learned about being an instructional leader and an effective principal.

4. *You will be able to grow emotionally and psychologically yourself as you gain the confidence to deal with your own personal fears of ineptitude and failure.* The principalship is a lonely job, and the most effective principals have discovered that the power to promote change in staff, students, and parents comes only through self-understanding and self-management. If you want to change the behavior of others, begin by changing your own behavior.

Voices of Experience

Several principals, both new and experienced veterans, talk about their greatest fears and challenges in the area of counseling and consulting. Can you relate to their experiences?

Karyn feels quite confident about her ability to communicate with children; she has recently been a successful and highly motivating classroom teacher. However, she feels most unprepared for handling parental complaints regarding teachers with whom she once worked:

> I dread having to defend or explain what one of my staff members is doing. As a teacher I had sort of a "hear no evil, see no evil" attitude, but now that I'm visiting in classrooms and actually see what's going on, I know a lot of change is needed. I'm not sure how I'm going to handle this issue. How can I be supportive and still hold teachers accountable?

Paolo, a veteran of principalships in several different schools, is a caring and warm person who hates conflict and confrontation. He tends to avoid talking about unpleasant topics or dealing with sensitive issues:

> I have a hard time with people who are negative. The minute somebody brings a problem to me, my stomach tightens up and I begin to feel powerless. I never know what to say and somehow I end up feeling like I'm to blame for the problem.

Susan describes her ambivalence when encountering a child who is being neglected or abused at home:

> I know what I am supposed to do: Report the situation to protective services. But sometimes things aren't so clear. What happens to the child after I do that? Maybe I'll just make things worse. I hope I have the courage to do what is right.

Tanya worries about her visibility in the principalship; the weight of the leadership mantle weighs heavily on her shoulders:

> It's very scary to think that everything I do and say is watched so closely. I remember well the conversations we used to have in the teachers lounge, always talking about the principal's latest harebrained scheme, or even the mismatched outfit he was wearing that day. Now that I'm the principal, I feel like I exist in a goldfish bowl. I know I'm supposed to be a role model but sometimes I don't even feel like I'm a grown-up myself.

Nick has been in the principalship for 3 years and wonders if he will ever learn to disconnect from the intense emotional problems that he encounters daily:

> The challenge for me is to be able to save enough of myself for my family when I get home. Some of these kids and parents are just so messed up and so needy—they need so much attention. If I'm going to last very long, I know I will have to back off, to separate their problems from my own.

Michael is a high-energy, outspoken classroom veteran. Named teacher of the year in his state, he's carried his presence and reputation into the principalship:

> I worry that I don't have the patience to deal with people who can't get the job done. There's so much whining that absolutely incenses me. I'm not sure I can continue to handle working with people who don't have the same commitment to excellence that I have.

Nila considers herself oversensitive to criticism and overly cautious about everything she says and does. She admits that these problems cloud her ability to counsel and consult effectively:

> I become obsessed with saying the "right" thing the "right" way. I don't want to hurt or embarrass anyone. Then I end up not doing or saying anything at all because I don't want to make any mistakes.

We suspect that some of these voices sound familiar to you, that perhaps you've heard them whispering inside your own head. You experience similar feelings of fear, inadequacy, impatience, and hypersensitivity. Acquiring a repertoire of counseling skills, however, can help you surmount these feelings and propel you to greater effectiveness as a communicator and leader. That is the wonder and power of this training: As you become more skilled and accomplished as a helper of others, you will become more proficient at applying what you know to your own life.

Life Inside the School

Education is, first and foremost, a helping profession. As the leader of your school, you are responsible for setting the tone, creating the culture, and tending to the climate of your school. While structuring a learning environment, the principal has to be aware of students' physical, emotional, and social needs, as well as their intellectual needs. The principal must ensure that all teachers create a pleasant atmosphere in their classrooms where students will be safe physically and secure psychologically to explore the world of ideas. From the first moment a new family arrives to enroll in your school, the trust- and rapport-building process begins. Although you may not physically process the paperwork or even be on hand to extend a personal welcome, the tone you set and the expectations you establish for office personnel will determine whether students and parents feel welcomed and affirmed from their first encounter with your school. The climate of respect and caring that engenders effective teaching from every teacher and learning for all students begins at the top. Your staff members, students, and parents will respond to your behavior and model what they see. If you are positive and constructive, they will be. If you expect tolerance and cooperation in the classroom, faculty workroom, and the PTO board meetings, you will get it. You will get what you expect, but only if you "walk your talk."

In addition to providing leadership and overall direction to the building, the principal needs to know and be involved in the lives of staff, students, and parents. In the case of faculty, the principal must be aware of the instructional strengths and weaknesses of each staff member and how the daily ups and downs of their lives are affecting not only their classroom performance but their interactions with fellow staff members. The school family experiences birth, death, illness, divorce, abuse, alcoholism, mental illness, infertility, financial difficulties, and the challenges of blended families. And those are just the staff members' problems. When you add to the mix these same problems multiplied by the number of parents and students in your school, the needs are tremendous.

Knowledge is power, however. The principal must know every teacher well—his or her instructional strengths and challenges, personal goals, and emotional needs. The principal must be ready to console the teacher who has suffered a miscarriage, the coach whose wife has deserted him, or the speech pathologist who has been diagnosed with terminal cancer. The principal must be ready to counsel an ineffective staff member on the wisdom of choosing another career path. The principal must be available to share a lunch at McDonald's with a student who has fulfilled the contract they developed together. To ignore these human needs to pursue administrative expedience will ignore the power of the human connection to bring about positive change for everyone.

The principal must further know every student and parent by name. This process will, of course, take longer in a larger school, but the goal is complete mastery and recall. The power and respect that is derived by remembering and calling students and parents by name is inestimable. Every child in your school will walk taller after being called by name. Imagine your surprise if you were to encounter the president of the university from which you graduated at a meeting and he or she called you by name. A child will experience that same burst of pride and an identical touch of astonishment that he or she was important enough to be noticed. Parents will feel affirmed when you remember who they are, and you'll reap even further benefits if you can talk about their child(ren) by name.

Finally, the principal must offer support, encouragement, and even direct intervention to many children whose special needs require teamwork and involvement by many professionals—to Dylan, whose struggle to find some measure of control over his troubled life has resulted in a complete work stoppage; to Amy, whose brother was killed by a hit-and-run driver; to Brian, whose dad moved out of the house last week; and to Susan, who is stealing candy and chips from her classmates' lunches. Changing friendships, fear of failure, family conflicts, and other issues occupy the minds of students. Understanding these issues is paramount, and playing a part in helping your students cope and surmount their challenges will empower your teachers to do the same.

At the same time, the principal must pay attention to external events that can be disruptive. A heated collective bargaining episode for teachers, a change in parking and pick-up regulations for parents, the suicide of a classmate for students—each has the potential to explode into a major issue if not handled appropriately.

Change interrupts the learning process, even when it is carefully planned. A crisis in the community will take precedence over any well-conceived lesson plan. In several cities, for example, riots have distracted kids from concentrating on relatively less important priorities such as homework. Children needed to be reassured that they were safe and nothing would harm them. They talked about the impact of violence, for example, in one city, how far they had to go to get food stamps after the welfare office had been burned. Immediate needs had to be addressed. Similarly, students in another town talked about depression, loneliness, and the responsibilities of friendship after one student tried to commit suicide.

The Principal as Facilitator and Manager

The principal's attendance at all meetings involving students and their needs is critical. Knowledge is power. The power of the pupil personnel services team, the teacher assistance team, and the resources of special educators can only be unleashed to their fullest extent if the principal is supportive, involved, and engaged in what is happening. Your interaction with and cultivation of counselors, social workers, and school psychologists, as well as special and remedial educators, will have a threefold benefit: (a) You will be able to learn an enormous amount about many disciplines that will assist you personally in your counseling and consulting efforts; (b) you will be aware of the resources at your fingertips to assist with difficult situations you may encounter; and (c) you will gain the respect, admiration, and complete cooperation of your staff as they perceive the respect and support you offer to them.

Relationships with staff, students, and parents are always evolving. Our goal is to provide you with the inspiration and motivation to develop the interpersonal skills so vital for the effective principal. Perhaps you will develop a clearer idea of what will be expected of you if you watch over the shoulder of one professional who goes about fulfilling her daily roles as a principal.

A Day in the Life

As Mrs. O'Connell opens the door to her car and prepares to gather her laptop and briefcase, she catches a glimpse of a child darting behind a tree on the playground. The rules are clear about arrival time at school and so she goes to investigate this early bird. She suspects it may be Jamie, whose mother leaves for work before he even wakes up. The wind-swept and frigid playground is preferable to the loneliness of his apartment. Mrs. O'Connell sighs. The paperwork she had anticipated completing before her staff begins to arrive must wait as she talks with Jamie.

It is 7:00 a.m. and Mrs. O'Connell, elementary school principal extraordinaire, is beginning the first of several hundred interactions she will have throughout the day with staff members, students, parents, and colleagues. The balancing act that constitutes her day often resembles the circus act in which the juggler keeps multiple plates spinning with careful attention to timing and speed. After a brief conversation with Jamie, she settles him in the outer office with a library book to occupy his attention and some snack crackers to fill his empty stomach.

With a fresh cup of coffee in hand, she mentally reviews what lies ahead—besides her usual administrative responsibilities. She knows that the first challenge of the day will be a meeting with the Travis family. Lucas has received a detention from the art teacher for hitting a classmate. His family is protesting his innocence and will be here to plead their case. Travis has his parents wound around his little finger. The challenge will be to help them understand what has been going on and what is best for their son. Before that can happen, however, she knows that the parents must feel heard and understood.

She will need to talk to the fifth-grade teacher about a new student who is enrolling. There are behavioral concerns, and although the ideal placement for the student would be with Mr. Snider, the disparity in enrollment between the two classes could be cause for a union grievance. She needs to travel across town to attend the staffing of a student who is being exited from a special education placement. She has also agreed to have lunch in her office with the kindergarten and first-grade teachers to discuss some philosophical differences they have regarding beginning reading instruction.

The lead teacher at sixth grade is going through a divorce, so she knows that she'll have to do some creative listening before Amy Escobedo will be ready to talk curriculum and instruction at their afternoon planning meeting. Also, she has been alerted that the fire chief will be by for an all-school fire drill and the annual inspection of the building. Mrs. O'Connell breathes deeply and counts to 10. The fire chief taxes her counseling skills to the limit. He's a bit confrontational and argumentative, believing that every school is on the verge of going up in flames and that learning would best take place if he was the one in charge of things.

In addition to these planned encounters, Mrs. O'Connell will also deal with a fight on the playground over a soccer game; a parent whose child refuses to come to school; a discussion with the social chairman of the faculty over her failure to send flowers to another staff member during her recent hospitalization; the custodian and lunchroom supervisor, who demand that something be done about the manners of today's children; the tracking down of a truant student and coaxing him back to school; the district's buildings and grounds manager, who can't understand the priority of filling a gaping hole left by utility workers; the arrival of the PTO president, who has a fabulous idea for a fundraiser that needs a decision immediately; and her secretary's refusal to listen to one more word of abuse from the teaching staff.

As you follow Mrs. O'Connell through an all-too-typical day, you notice the great number of people she comes into contact with and the variety of situations in which she uses her interpersonal skills. One moment she is talking to a student who is lonely and left out; in the next she is counseling a parent whose son has been arrested for shoplifting. She must shift gears almost effortlessly as she moves from affirming a first grader who arrives to demonstrate his newly learned decoding skills to a challenging evaluation conference that could result in a teacher dismissal. The day is packed with interactions as people turn to her for guidance and as she lets others know she cares about what is happening to them.

Whether you like it or not, whether you are prepared or not, everybody wants the principal's help—students, staff, parents, even people in the community who see you as a civic leader. They ask for help in sorting out values as well as in evaluating the ethics of the situations they face. They come to share the events that take place in their lives, both joyous and sad. They look to you for help in solving problems.

The ways you respond to these situations and the fluency and ease with which you switch the multiple hats you wear will profoundly affect the quality of the educational experiences found in your school, as well as your own job satisfaction. Your knowledge of counseling skills will affect your relationships with the children with whom you work, the staff members with whom you share common goals and experiences at school, the parents who have entrusted their children to your care, your friendships and affiliations with colleagues, and even the quality of intimacy with the people you love the most.

Suggested Activities

1. What aspects of the principal's counseling and consulting roles do you find to be most challenging? What types of interaction/situations do you feel most unprepared for? After reflecting on these questions, (a) write down your responses and put the pages in a safe place where you can reread what you wrote several years from now, and (b) share your reactions in a group of peers meeting to discuss their concerns.

2. Give a writing assignment to the students in your school to answer this question: What does the principal do? Their responses will enlighten, encourage, and inform you about your own multiple roles. Pay special attention to what they *don't* say about you that you wish they would.

3. Ask your staff members to complete this brief three-question assessment:
   a. What am I doing as a principal that you would like me to continue doing?
   b. What am I doing that you would like me to stop doing?
   c. What else could I do to increase my effectiveness as a principal?

   The task of collecting, collating, and summarizing the assessments should be given to two or three trusted teachers, who will then sit down with you to explain and discuss the results. Pay special attention to the requests involving your counseling and consulting skills.

Suggested Readings

Brock, B. (1997). *From first-year to first-rate*. Thousand Oaks, CA: Corwin.

Corey, M. S., & Corey, G. (1998). *Becoming a helper* (3rd ed.). Pacific Grove, CA: Brooks/Cole.

Covey, S. (1989). *Seven habits of highly effective people.* New York: Simon & Schuster.

Hazler, R. J. (1998). *Helping in the hallways: Advanced strategies for enhancing school relationships.* Thousand Oaks, CA: Corwin.

Ram Das, & Gorman, P. (1985). *How can I help? Stories and reflections on service.* New York: Knopf.

Wegela, K. K. (1990). *How to be a help instead of a nuisance.* Boston: Shambhala.

2

Assessing Problems

The first step in applying counseling and consulting skills, whether with students, staff, or parents, is learning how to recognize problems. Assessment is an important part of any helper's role. But make no mistake: It's a daunting task.

For example, how would you assess Curt? He's a lanky third grader who could pass for much older but his emotional maturity doesn't begin to match his size. Lately, he's been complaining of stomachaches. They seem to arrive just after lunch, specifically during math class. He has visited the pediatrician, who pronounced him physically fit, but that doesn't stop him from frequent trips to the nurse. Is Curt suffering from math anxiety, depression, allergies to whole wheat bread, school phobia, or some other mysterious malady? Does he need empathy, a pep talk, academic support, a complete medical workup, or a referral to a psychologist? While we're debating what Curt needs, he's wearing out his welcome in the health office.

Lots of Problems, Some of Them Tricky Ones

You are undoubtedly familiar with a substantial number of children's difficulties, including academic underachievement, cognitive deficits, learning disabilities, behavioral problems, and signs of child abuse. Yet these areas of difficulty represent, proportionately, only a small segment of what children struggle with in their daily lives. They are fighting to establish themselves as autonomous, confident, and competent human beings. They are working through a number of developmental transitions related to achieving physical, cognitive, emotional, and moral maturity. They are recovering from the stresses and strains of family and peer pressure, trying desperately to find a place in the world where they belong. And these are only the predictable and normal problems of adjustment that children encounter.

About one in five students in your school is suffering from emotional difficulties not considered part of normal childhood adjustment. These children are highly anxious, so much so that they develop psychosomatic illnesses and stress-related symptoms such as chronic headaches, stomachaches, ulcers, and insomnia. Depression is also quite common among school-age children, a condition that often goes overlooked because these students tend to be withdrawn, passive, and listless—not the sort to draw attention to themselves. Some of these students are potentially suicidal and spend an inordinate amount of time planning their own demise, all while staring blankly at the blackboard. Still other children are hiding symptoms of drug abuse or eating disorders.

You will, of course, already have noticed those who have the more dramatic signs of severe personality disorders, but the vast majority of children's problems are overlooked by educators who are not trained to notice their warning signs.

By the way, Curt fooled all the experts. The principal thought he had a touch of school phobia. Curt's mom decided he was allergic to food dyes and began to tinker with his diet. The family doctor thought Curt was a normal kid going through one of those phases that all kids go through. His teacher thought Curt was making it all up because he didn't want to learn his multiplication facts. After weeks of trying to figure out Curt's problem, he doubled over in pain and was rushed to the hospital for an emergency appendectomy. He had a speedy recovery and returned to school where he quickly caught up with the class and even learned his multiplication facts.

Other Problems to Face

Assessing problems in staff and parents can often be more baffling than those of students. Adults are more skilled at dissembling and more sophisticated in disguising their symptoms. They are susceptible to the same emotional difficulties that bother many children, plus they must confront issues related to job and family responsibility, financial pressures, and declining health.

The teachers, parents, and staff members you encounter on a daily basis are continually going in and out of personal crises, some of them related to their work in the school, but just as many connected to things at home. You are the person many will confide in when they suspect a spouse is having an affair, a bankruptcy is impending, one of their kids has run away from home, they've been diagnosed with a chronic or terminal illness, or many of the developmental transitions that you are facing as well: fear of aging, fear of failure, fears that much of their hard work, ultimately, doesn't really matter.

Marilyn Smith is the PTO treasurer. The principal has always found her to be competent, resourceful, and a willing worker, but lately she has skipped some meetings and several outstanding bills are overdue. More often than not, the answering machine picks up messages and Marilyn rarely returns a phone call. Are the Smiths experiencing marital difficulties? Has Marilyn absconded with the PTO treasury? Is she physically ill? Experiencing a problem with alcohol? Depressed? Or all of the above. While we are discussing the exact nature of Marilyn's problem, the PTO was served with a collection notice.

For your information, Marilyn Smith was recently diagnosed with multiple sclerosis. Her husband, unglued by the news, moved out. Marilyn was understandably depressed, borrowed some money from the treasury to pay the mortgage, and started drinking herself to sleep at night. School personnel were able to help Marilyn with referrals to various agencies and designed a plan for her to repay the funds. A new PTO treasurer was appointed. But none of this happened without the principal conducting an elaborate assessment of the various issues, intervening systematically in a variety of ways.

Bryan Marks, fifth-grade teacher, had always been a mercurial person. But his recent mood swings have left the children in his class, as well as his intermediate team members, wondering "which Bryan" will show up today. Whenever the principal observes his teaching, however, he pulls the proverbial rabbit out the hat and dazzles with magic. He is unquestionably a gifted teacher. One group of parents adores Bryan for his elaborate interdisciplinary units and off-beat approaches. Another group of parents has seen a different side of Bryan, his defensive, angry, cynical side. When parents love Bryan, he loves them back, showering them with compliments and telephone calls. But if you question his methods or motives, expect to get the cold shoulder. Is Bryan a manic-depressive? Is he prone to some type of personality disorder? Might there even be some sort of brain problem that affects his moods? Does he have a problem with drug abuse? Could excessive drinking be responsible for his behavior? While we are contemplating just who the "real" Bryan Marks is, the students in his classroom are learning more about how to navigate the moods of Mr. Marks than they are about reading and math.

For your information, Bryan Marks had a drug problem. Unfortunately, he was also selling drugs to former students. It took a lot of thorough investigation on the principal's part to figure out what was going on, eliminate some possibilities, and consider the most likely scenario. Mr. Marks was terminated under an agreement in which the district health plan paid for his rehabilitation.

The Assessment Process

The most critical component of any intervention plan designed to help individuals in need is to accurately assess the nature of their difficulties. What are the underlying reasons for their behavior? As you have seen from our examples, there are always several possible explanations. A given individual's behavior could mean any number of things—that he is chronically shy, that he is depressed, that he feels alienated and lonely, that he suffers from a personality disorder in which he is disconnected from the human race, that he is on drugs or overmedicated, that he is physically ill or sleep deprived, perhaps even that he is a member of a culture in which his behavior is considered socially appropriate. Each of these possible diagnoses would suggest a different method of intervention and a different professional with whom you might consult for help.

It is not enough to sense that something is wrong with a child or an adult; you must also have a rough idea of what is going on before you can take appropriate action. This process of systematically observing behavior, determining if it indicates some underlying difficulty, narrowing down the possibilities to a few reasonable hypotheses, and then initiating some form of action resembles the differential diagnostic methods of physicians and psychologists. Your job is to figure out if indeed there is a serious problem, and if so, what to do about it.

Essentially, you will be asking yourself a series of questions:

- What is unusual about this person's behavior?
- Is there a pattern to what I have observed?
- What information do I need to make an informed judgment?
- Who might I contact to collect this background?
- What are the risks of waiting longer to figure out what is going on?
- Does this person seem to be in any imminent danger?
- What can I do to build a better relationship with this person?
- Who can I consult about this case?

It is certainly beyond the scope of your role as a principal to be able to accurately diagnose a host of emotional disorders, be able to differentiate them from one another, and then prescribe corresponding treatments. However, it is perfectly reasonable that with added training and supervised experience, you would become proficient in recognizing some of the signs of an individual who is in trouble. We will review some of the more common disorders and difficulties you will encounter, both with children and adults; list the most prevalent symptoms you might observe; and then mention the usual treatment strategies so that you can take appropriate action or make informed referrals.

Generalized Anxiety

Description: Excessive worry and apprehension over things that are out of one's control or in which the reaction is exaggerated beyond what is reasonable.

Examples: A child agonizes continuously over school, sports, and social performance. He expresses persistent concern over possible harm that may befall his parents and so is reluctant to separate from them. A teacher constantly seeks out the principal for guidance, clarification, and direction, seemingly unable to make any decisions on his own. A parent hovers over her child, unable to keep from dropping in the classroom several times a day to make sure he's OK.

Symptoms: Nausea, stomachaches, headaches, sweating, dry mouth, frequent urination, dizziness, agitation, restlessness, irritability.

Usual interventions: Give lots of reassurance, use relaxation training and stress management, provide an opportunity to talk about fears and learn alternative ways to handle them, refer for counseling, make a referral to rule out associated physical maladies.

Phobic Disorders

Description: Avoidant and anxious responses to specific situations, such as being in open spaces (agoraphobia); separating from a parent (separation anxiety); social situations (social phobia); or spiders, snakes, high places, and so on (simple phobia).

Examples: A child develops a persistent refusal to go to school after an embarrassing experience. She refuses to leave her parent's side when she is forcibly dragged away from home. A parent keeps canceling appointments for parent-teacher conferences, afraid to leave her apartment.

Symptoms: Persistent fears, physical sensations (sweating, heart palpitations, trembling, nausea, numbness, dizziness), avoidance of threatening stimulus.

Usual interventions: Principals will want to work very closely with a counselor or psychologist who can design a treatment program containing cognitive and behavioral components. Family counseling may be indicated. In school phobia cases, gradual desensitization is introduced. Teachers can be helpful by creating a supportive atmosphere.

Depression

Description: A pervasive mood disorder in which the individual feels sad and withdrawn, with muted affect. There are several different kinds of depression: *endogenous depression* is a biologically based disorder that is caused by a neurochemical imbalance in the body; *dysthymia* is another chronic but less serious mood disorder in which there is no serious disruption of sleep, appetite, or daily functioning; *reactive depression* is an acute response to some crisis or distressing situation (grief, adjustment to life changes, etc.).

Examples: A child has recently moved to the district from another city. He appears very quiet, reticent, and withdrawn. Sometimes you can see tears welling up in his eyes. He keeps to himself mostly and does not initiate interaction with other children. A teacher never smiles in her classroom, and her students frequently complain that she doesn't like them. A parent seems powerless to respond to any requests for follow-through at home and often forgets to sign homework notices.

Symptoms: In mild cases: sadness following an identifiable stressful event that precipitated the symptoms, low energy, poor concentration, low self-esteem, no history of recurrent episodes. In severe cases: disruption of normal functioning, appetite loss, sleep disruption, weight loss or gain, listlessness, abject hopelessness, rumination, suicidal thoughts and possible intent.

Usual interventions: Mild, reactive depression responds quite well to supportive relationships in which the individual has the opportunity to express feelings and learn alternative ways of thinking about his or her predicament. Time is usually the best healer.

Severe endogenous depression, on the other hand, is potentially life threatening without intervention. In some cases, intensive psychotherapy in addition to medication is required. The principal can play a crucial role by making sure the individual does receive expert help.

Suicide Potential

Although it is relatively common for children (and adults) to contemplate suicide during times of stress, here are some specific warning signs to watch for that indicate the potential for serious intent:

1. Toward the end of the school year, when risks increase (applicable to students, teachers, and parents alike)
2. Use of drugs or alcohol
3. Extensive preoccupation with death fantasies

4. Absence of a support system

5. Evidence that the individual has a specific plan as to how he or she would do it

6. Evidence that the individual has the means available to carry out the plan (a loaded gun or bottle of sleeping pills in the home)

7. A history of self-destructive acts

8. A gesture on the part of the individual that may be interpreted as a cry for help

9. A history of a relative having killed himself or herself (providing a model of an acceptable way out)

10. Significant mood changes from depression to elation

11. Noticeable changes in an individual's appearance or performance

Also important to keep in mind: Urban dwellers are at greater risk than rural folks, and certain minority groups (Native Americans) have higher than average suicide rates.

Prevention is critically important. Principals can be most helpful by creating an atmosphere in their school in which everyone is responsible for everyone else's welfare. Almost 90% of children who attempt suicide tell somebody of their intent—a friend, a parent, a teacher. By alerting children to the risk, we can recruit their assistance in preventing tragedy. This is the case not only with self-destructive acts but also those recent instances in which children have resorted to inflicting extreme violence on others.

Adults may be less open in providing obvious clues. Keep in mind, however, that predicting suicidal acts is not an exact science; it is better to be cautious and conservative and consult a counselor when you suspect an individual is at risk.

Attention Deficit Hyperactivity Disorder

Description: High degrees of impulsivity, unrestrained energy, and inattention that are well outside the norm. The behavior is manifested in a number of settings: in school, at home, and work. Furthermore, it seriously impairs the individual's ability to concentrate or perform assigned tasks.

Examples: A child is performing poorly in school in spite of an apparent high degree of intelligence. She almost always appears restless, practically vibrating with energy as her attention wanders from one thing to another without pause. The more concentration that is required for a particular task in school, the more frustrated she becomes. The teacher is highly creative and energetic but seldom completes assigned tasks, remembers deadlines, or keeps appointments. She depends on others to remind and nag her. The parent is supportive, well intentioned, and always promises he will help. He never follows through, however. He does not keep appointments and is seemingly incapable of helping his child maintain structure.

Symptoms: Restless or fidgeting behavior, difficulty staying in one place for a period of time, easily distracted, impulsive behavior, wandering attention from assigned tasks that are rarely completed, talks excessively or constantly interrupts others, has difficulty listening to and following instructions.

Usual interventions: Structured individual assignments that are within the person's threshold of attentiveness; tight external boundaries; medication for severe cases.

Conduct Disorder

Description: A persistent pattern of abusing the rights of others with little regard for established rules. This person will appear unduly aggressive, even cruel in his or her destructive, violent, or antisocial behavior.

Example: A child explodes with temper tantrums when he does not get his way. He is provocative and seems oblivious to other children's feelings. He is often discovered to be starting fights, stealing others' things, doing anything to get his way. Furthermore, he shows no guilt or remorse over his actions. He feels entitled to get his way whenever he wants and views others as his personal slaves.

In the case of parents or teachers who display extreme abusive or disruptive behavior, they have "grown" into an adult type of personality disorder (narcissistic, borderline, sociopathic, etc.) in which they appear to lack the capacity for empathy or concern for others. They tend to be exploitative, manipulative, and self-centered. You will notice especially ways that they resent any authority figure such as a principal, working to undermine you behind your back or humiliate you to yourself. In many cases, they may have exhibited conduct disorders as children that were never checked.

Symptoms: A pattern of cruelty toward animals or other age mates; participation in frequent fights; deliberate destruction of others' property; either alone or as a leader of others, he or she initiates aggressive acts.

Usual interventions: Set very strict boundaries with immediate enforcement of consequences for noncompliance with rules; improve frustration tolerance through gradual presentation of more challenging tasks; family counseling to work on consistent parenting; inpatient treatment for severe cases.

Oppositional Disorder

Description: A less severe version of a conduct disorder in which the child shows a pattern of being hostile, defiant, and uncooperative. This behavior is not necessarily universal but may appear only in certain settings (at home, in certain classes, when around certain people, in response to certain stimuli). This child does show some concern for others' rights and does not deliberately hurt others in attempts to protect herself.

Example: A child appears surly, hostile, even ferocious in her opposition to you and things you ask of her. When you ask her to do something, she outright refuses, or sometimes even does the exact opposite. You can hear her swear at you behind your back and feel her disdain for you and everything you stand for.

You would observe similar parents with oppositional parents and teachers who challenge you consistently, often without apparent motive or reason. They seem to thrive on the power they feel getting underneath your skin.

Symptoms: Frequent loss of temper; situational arguments with authority figures; a pattern of defiance, vindictiveness, and annoying others; common swearing and dramatic rebellion.

Usual interventions: Set limits and enforce them without retribution; examine your own contributions to precipitating the oppositional behavior; schedule individual conferences to confront the behavior nondefensively and work on a more empathic relationship. Unlike those suffering from conduct disorders, these children and adults respond quite well to systematic attempts to improve self-esteem, frustration tolerance, emotional control, and aggression. They also respond well to counseling because they must develop cooperative relationships with an authority figure during the process.

Eating Disorders

Description: A disturbance in eating behavior characterized by significant weight loss and obsession with food (anorexia nervosa); episodes of binging and forced vomiting (bulimia); or persistent eating of nonnutritious substances such as paint, chalk, plaster, paper, leaves, and so on (pica).

Example: You have noticed that one of the teachers is as "skinny as a rail," yet you have occasionally overheard her remark to friends how fat she is. She has low self-esteem. You recall that she was once much heavier and began to lose weight after her relationship with a boyfriend ended.

Symptoms: Anorexia nervosa and bulimia occur almost exclusively among girls and young women; perfectionistic behavior; mild obesity before onset of weight loss; excessive concern for food but poor eating habits; distorted body image.

Usual interventions: Because in virtually all cases the person's friends and family know about her unusual eating habits, principals can do a lot to educate others on the signs of trouble and the dangerous consequences of these disorders. In severe cases, eating disorders are potentially lethal without hospitalization. In more moderate cases, family counseling and behavior modification are often successful.

Substance Abuse Disorders

Description: The addiction to, dependence on, or habitual use of alcohol, marijuana, cocaine, barbiturates, amphetamines, or other substances to the extent that normal functioning is impaired.

Examples: A child in class repeatedly falls asleep and appears lethargic when he is awake. His eyes sometimes appear glassy, his speech slurred. There has been a noticeable change in his behavior and academic performance over the course of several weeks. You happen to know that he spends a lot of time in the company of his older siblings and their friends, who are frequent drug users.

One of the teachers has been exhibiting erratic attendance patterns, beginning after the death of his mother. At first, it seemed that he was dealing with grief alone, but lately his appearance seems disheveled and his behavior unpredictable. He is always chewing on breath mints.

Symptoms: Frequent use of a psychoactive substance in increasing amounts; little control over the amount and frequency of substance that is ingested; a lot of time spent thinking about the drug; social and school activities disrupted; impairment in functioning that may be manifested in slurred speech, shaky gait, glassy or bloodshot eyes, irritability, hyperactivity, or lethargy.

Usual interventions: A supportive relationship can be a catalyst for a student, teacher, or parent to break away from self-destructive habits. The treatment of these problems is very difficult because they involve both a physical habit or addiction and social reinforcement among one's peer group. Referral to a specialist in substance abuse disorders is usually indicated because the person may need fairly drastic disruption of his or her usual life routines to recover fully. Brief hospitalization is often suggested along with family counseling, individual counseling, and reeducation. By far, prevention is the best treatment, and principals play a major role in addressing the risks before behavior gets out of hand.

Obsessive-Compulsive Disorder

Description: Recurrent thoughts (obsessions) or repetitive behaviors (compulsions) beyond one's control. They are usually senseless ideas or actions that represent attempts to ward off other concerns through ritualistic action.

Example: A child meticulously arranges every aspect of her desk before she will attempt any project. She is insistent that everything be absolutely in its correct place and refuses to do any work unless everything is in order. She rarely completes any of her work because of her inordinate concern for arranging materials.

Symptoms: Repetitive behavior or recurrent thoughts that keep anxiety under control; images or impulses are intrusive and render the person at least minimally dysfunctional.

Usual interventions: The earlier the obsessive thinking or compulsive behavior is detected, the greater the likelihood that it can be treated; behavior therapy is the preferred intervention; medication is also sometimes effective.

Somatization Disorder

Description: A long-standing series of physical complaints without any apparent organic cause. This disorder represents the body's attempt to metabolize stress. The child is distressed by the symptoms and is not faking them.

Example: A child constantly complains of stomachaches. He has been taken to a number of specialists but they have found no cause for the trouble.

Symptoms: Preoccupation with some problem in the body for which there is no known physical cause. Common symptoms include abdominal pain, back pain, or headaches.

Usual interventions: Rule out completely the possibility of any medical condition; focus on improving functioning in school and with friends rather than on symptoms themselves; stress reduction strategies; referral to a counselor or psychologist for individual and/or family therapy to explore sources of anxiety.

Factitious Disorder

Description: Intentional manufacture of physical problems to gain attention or sympathy, to assume a sick role, or to escape some obligation.

Example: A child has missed a lot of school because of illnesses. One day she complained of stomach pains and wished to go home.

You told her to wait a little while to see if she felt any better. You then caught her unobtrusively trying to make herself vomit.

Symptoms: A persistent pattern of deliberately feigned physical symptoms; a personality that is demanding and manipulative; high need for attention.

Usual interventions: Eliminate consequences the child is enjoying as a result of malingering; refer to individual and family counseling to get at sources of need for attention.

Sexual Abuse

Description: The incidence of sexual abuse has been estimated as high as 25% of all girls; although the frequency is less among boys, it is still a major problem; most of these occurrences go unreported and significantly affect a child's self-esteem, development, and school performance.

Example: A child cringes when you softly touch her arm to offer comfort. You have observed that this is her usual response to any adult who comes too close to her.

Symptoms: Fear of adults, especially own parents; reluctance to go home; withdrawal or regressive behavior; complaints of frequent nightmares; secretiveness about family life; reported stories of being touched inappropriately.

Usual interventions: Suspected sexual abuse must be reported to the authorities, triggering an investigation; treatment usually consists of family counseling, with separate treatment for the perpetrator(s); principals are instrumental in helping the child develop a safe, trusting relationship with a caring adult; the child is usually seen in individual counseling to work on issues related to betrayal, self-esteem, and accompanying guilt. Principals can help by creating a safe "family environment" in the school.

Adjustment Disorders

Description: Stressful reactions to some recent event in the person's life (such as a death in the family, relocation, illness, or relationship problem).

Examples: Formerly a cheerful and very good student, a child became surly, uncooperative, and withdrawn after being informed his parents were getting a divorce. A teacher becomes extremely anxious and fearful after surviving a car accident with only minor injuries. A parent who had previously been very cheerful and optimistic has become withdrawn and passive after losing her job.

Symptoms: Anxiety, depression, withdrawal, behavioral changes, physical complaints, or reduced academic performance immediately following an identifiable stressful event in the person's life.

Usual interventions: These are the kinds of difficulties that respond best to a principal's empathic concern. The majority of people will improve on their own if provided the time and opportunity to do so. Referral to a counselor can hasten the recovery period, as can participation in support groups. Principals can often be of tremendous assistance in providing a setting for people to talk about what is bothering them and to feel understood.

Most often, you will see this last category of emotional concerns. Fortunately, these emotional concerns are also the kinds of difficulties that respond best to a principal moderately skilled in helping strategies. With some training, you can make a positive difference in a relatively short period of time.

Suggested Activities

1. Among the various diagnostic entities described in this chapter, it's likely that a few of them will seem familiar to you, not only in other people you have observed but also in yourself. Do an honest assessment of yourself, noting which areas you have struggled with the most.

2. Think about the students, parents, and teachers you have come into contact with in the past year. Try to re-create an inventory of all the various problems you have personally witnessed that have been described in this chapter.

3. Conduct an interview with a partner in which you attempt to conduct a comprehensive assessment of strengths and weaknesses.

Suggested Readings

Capuzzi, D., & Gross, D. (1996). *Youth at risk: A prevention resource for counselors, teachers, and parents* (2nd ed.). Alexandria, VA: American Counseling Association.

Jones, W. P. (1997). *Deciphering the diagnostic codes: A guide for school counselors.* Thousand Oaks, CA: Corwin.

Kottler, J. A. (1992). *Compassionate therapy: Working with difficult clients.* San Francisco: Jossey-Bass.

Morrison, J. (1995). *DSM-IV made easy: The clinician's guide to diagnosis.* New York: Guilford.

Seligman, L. (1998). *Selecting effective treatments* (2nd ed.). San Francisco: Jossey-Bass.

3

Understanding the Process of Helping

Once you have been able to assess accurately that a student, staff member, or parent is in need of help, and perhaps have been able to narrow down the choices to a few reasonable possibilities, you will be ready for the process of helping. In some cases, the appropriate action is to refer the individual to a specialist for more expert intervention; in most instances, however, you may very well be able to offer constructive help yourself. What you need to do is follow the systematic process described in this chapter and then apply the skills described in the following chapter.

Counseling Principles

It is not your job to do counseling on a regular basis or to act as a ready confidant for every needy person in the school family. You will not have the time, opportunity, or training to serve in those roles. But there will be daily instances in which someone will reach out to you for understanding, and some rudimentary background in several skills will allow you to help them. First are some basic ideas to keep in mind:

1. *You cannot learn helping skills by reading about them.* If you are serious about augmenting your repertoire of interpersonal skills, you must practice them.

2. *Being in a helping role is not natural.* In spite of what you may have heard otherwise, functioning as a counselor means doing a

number of things that are unnatural, such as being nonjudgmental and putting your own needs aside.

3. *You are dealing with concerns, not problems.* Problems imply there are solutions, even right ones, yet most often, personal issues have no single answers. Most people continue to struggle with the same issues (fear of failure, search for meaning, need for affirmation, etc.) their whole lives.

4. *Don't give advice.* By telling people what you think they should do with their lives, one of two things can happen, both of which can lead to negative consequences. First, if you think you know what is best for someone and you tell him or her what to do and the results are disastrous, you will get blamed for the rest of your life for being the one at fault. The only thing worse than giving bad advice is giving good advice. If what you tell people to do works out beautifully, then what they have learned is that when they don't know what to do in the future, they should consult someone else to tell them what to do. You, after all, have reinforced the idea that they are incapable of making decisions on their own.

5. *Don't try to do too much.* The most frequent difficulty that beginning counselors have is, ironically, trying to do too much. Remember, it is the individual's issue—all you can do is help the person feel that he or she is not alone, that you understand, and that you support the person's decision.

6. *Before you begin, slip into a "helping" mode.* Similar to meditation and other altered states of consciousness, helping another person involves focused concentration. When you decide to help someone, you are making a decision, temporarily, to clear your mind of all your own "stuff," to resist distractions, and to stay nonjudgmental about what you are hearing. Furthermore, except when individuals are in danger of hurting themselves or someone else, you are committed to keeping private communications confidential.

Things to remember before you start:

- Take a deep breath to clear your mind.
- Focus your concentration completely on this person in need.
- Avoid any distractions.
- Communicate your undivided attention nonverbally.
- Remain as neutral, nonjudgmental, and accepting as possible.

7. *Don't let yourself feel overwhelmed.* This is only a brief overview of material that would take you 2 years of full-time study in which to develop competency. It is neither realistic nor reasonable for you to expect to put all the ideas and skills presented to use. Our goal is merely to help you expand your current levels of interpersonal effectiveness. As you evolve in your career, you will find many opportunities for inservice training, workshops, graduate courses, tapes, and books that will help you become progressively more proficient in these skills.

Helping Attitudes

Although in this and the next chapter we are about to present you with the process and skills of helping, it is important to keep in mind that counseling relationships involve a lot more than mastery of expert techniques. There is a helping attitude that counselors adopt when in session, a state of mind that keeps them clear, focused, and receptive.

We just mentioned being nonjudgmental as one facet of a helping posture. Other features that have been demonstrated again and again as crucial to developing solid relationships are authenticity, genuineness, caring, respect, and compassion. These are not just words we give lip service to; these attitudes are the essence of what it means to make contact with and truly understand another human being.

Unlike the skills we present, you cannot "learn" these attitudes merely by practicing them. To feel caring and compassionate toward children, staff members, parents, or anyone, especially when they are going out of their way to be unlovable, you must make a major commitment. Your dedication is obvious because you have already chosen the profession of education.

Yet remember that the act of helping is not only an applied set of skills and techniques, it represents your attempt to bring comfort and constructive input to somebody who is struggling or in great pain.

An Integrative Approach to Counseling

You know that educators have long debated which is the best way to promote learning. You no doubt studied dozens of theories in your education classes, each of which presents an apparently unique explanation to account for how children learn. You have also been exposed to considerable difference of opinion as to what makes an effective leader. Some theorists suggest that qualities like charisma and vision are inborn; others posit the theory that the situation and the times create great leaders. Still others believe that leadership behaviors can be learned. The really confusing thing, however, is that each theory seems to present a measure of truth, even though they rely on different and even contradictory principles.

Debates about the "best way" are no less strident in the counseling field. There are as many as 400 different systems of helping that claim they have evidence indicating that their way of working is the best, that they have discovered "truth." Rather than concentrating on the unique features of different approaches, we focus on the elements that almost all practitioners would agree are important. Any generic helping approach, whether practiced by counselors, psychologists, psychiatrists, social workers, teachers, or witch doctors—whether in our culture or somewhere else—will have similar operative ingredients.

Altered states of consciousness. The object of all helping approaches, whether in teaching, counseling, or administrating, is to initiate perceptual changes and to influence thinking, feeling, and behavior. Efforts to accomplish these tasks are more likely to be successful if the person is in a receptive mode. This increased receptivity to influence takes place when someone is in a more suggestible mood, a state that can be created by anyone who constructs a helping environment that is conducive to change. There are things that you can do to increase your status, expertise, and power in the eyes of those you are called on to help and thereby guide them to be more receptive to what you have to offer.

Placebo effects. A universal aspect of any change process is influencing people's belief systems in such a way that they become convinced that the procedure will be successful. Doctors do this when they offer relatively benign medications with the accompaniment, "I know this will make you feel better." We do essentially the same thing when we are able to communicate to individuals that what we do works very well. By believing in our own power to be helpful, we offer hope and inspiration to people who have often given up: "I'm so glad you decided to come and speak with me. I have heard a number of others express similar concerns. I have no doubt that you will feel much better after we talk, and I just know that I can help you." This message has an almost hypnotic quality, communicating our belief that the process we offer does indeed work.

Therapeutic relationship. Of all the universal features that we will mention, the therapeutic relationship may be the most powerful factor of all. Most people strive for intimacy in their lives; each person wishes to be connected to and understood by others. Whereas long ago we all belonged to close-knit tribes of friends, relatives, and neighbors who were all concerned with one another, modern life offers a more fragmented, disconnected existence. Children hunger for close relationships, as do adults. One of the common elements of every helping system is an emphasis on creating an alliance that is open, trusting, accepting, and safe. This therapeutic relationship becomes intrinsically healing in some ways. It offers comfort and support. It motivates risk taking. It becomes the core for everything else we do in the helping process.

Cathartic process. Sigmund Freud discovered long ago that when people are given the opportunity to explore what is bothering them, to talk without interruption about their fears and concerns, they will feel much better afterward. Every counseling approach has cathartic processes built into it in which the individual is permitted and encouraged to talk about whatever is most troublesome. By developing just a few relationship-building skills, you will be able to capitalize on these last two elements exceedingly well.

Consciousness-raising. Any significant change means alterations in the way one looks at oneself, at others, and at the world. As a principal, you are particularly well suited to effect these kinds of changes. The position of leadership and respect you hold makes you a natural to use your influence to promote more self-understanding and self-discovery on the part of your students, teachers, and parents.

Reinforcement. Counseling uses the therapeutic relationship as a means by which to systematically shape more fully functioning behavior and to extinguish self-defeating actions. When the individual reports that for the first time he really understands why he has been having certain problems, we offer immediate support; likewise, when he engages in maladaptive behavior, we deliberately ignore or discourage those responses. In counseling sessions, this re-inforcement may often be quite subtle: As the individual speaks of feeling powerful and in control, we smile and nod, whereas when he acts passive and dependent, we appear more neutral and less sup-portive of this behavior. Of course, the challenge in applying any behavioral principles is to make clear that although we approve and disapprove of certain behavior, we always unconditionally continue to care for the individual.

Rehearsal. Counseling sessions provide particularly good oppor-tunities for individuals to practice new behaviors within the safety of the therapeutic relationship and with plenty of feedback. For ex-ample, a child who is complaining that nobody likes him can't seem to figure out a way to make friends with other students. You can help him rehearse conversational icebreakers that he can initiate later that day when he goes out for recess.

Principal: OK, so pretend that I'm someone you want to play with.

Child: I don't think I can do this. Nobody wants to meet me.

Principal: Are you saying that you don't even want to try?

Child: Well, I guess so.

Principal: You don't sound very convincing.

Child: Yes! Yes, I do want to try making friends.

Principal: (Slipping into the role of classmate.) Hey, what are you just standing around for over there?

Child: Um, I, ah, I just wanted to . . . I mean . . . oh, never mind.

Principal: (Offering support.) Well, that was a start anyway. This time, just say what you want to say. Don't worry about how he will respond.

As this coached dialogue continues, the boy is helped to articulate what is most important for him to communicate. He receives feed-back on strategies that he might try. Most important, he has the op-portunity to practice acting in more powerful ways, an experience that will serve him well in life even if the interaction with his class-mate does not work out as he would prefer.

The rehearsal strategy can be used with a teacher who is dreading a conference with a volatile parent or with a parent whose personal experiences in elementary school have left her unable to articulate her questions to an assertive teacher.

Task facilitation. One of the most important things we can ever do for the members of our school family is encourage them to try new ways of acting. Most approaches to counseling include helping people complete therapeutic tasks. Obviously, the child in the previous example has a tremendous amount of reluctance to initiating a social contact. If we can define a successful outcome as not so much getting one's way as trying to act courageously, then the child will feel better about himself no matter how his peer responds to his overture.

Each preceding element just reviewed is part of all counseling efforts, regardless of the theoretical persuasion of the practitioner. As we look in greater depth at exactly what is involved in a counseling encounter, keep in mind that this is a generic approach, one that most members of the profession would agree is somewhat universal. As you come to gain more experience and training, you may very well adapt this general approach to one that fits better with your personality, leadership style, and the specific needs of the individual.

A Review of the Counseling Process

The counseling process follows a series of logical and sequential stages, not unlike what you might invent intuitively from any problem-solving effort. Although these components are presented as if they were discrete parts, in fact the boundaries often overlap to the point where it's hard to determine which stage you're at. The important point is to have an overview of how helping takes place, the stages that individuals who are processing problems usually go through, and a blueprint for where you are headed once you identify your current position in the process.

Assessment. Before you can attempt any effort at being helpful you have to have some idea as to what is going on. Counselors and therapists call this the "identification of the presenting complaint," but actually it is simply a systematic effort to help an individual describe what is bothersome. It is also crucial to collect any important background information relevant to the concerns.

As you imagine yourself conducting this assessment, it will probably occur to you that there are a number of skills you would need that are probably not already part of your professional repertoire. The next chapter reviews in greater detail the particular skills required, but for now we will simply indicate which skills are important in the various stages. To begin, the counseling skills most often associated with an assessment are (a) asking open-ended questions, (b) reflecting the individual's feelings, and (c) clarifying the content of what is being presented.

Imagine that the child from our earlier example tells you he is upset because he doesn't have many friends. Immediately, you would think of a number of questions you want to ask; you need more information to be helpful to this person: What do you mean you don't have many friends? Who are you close to? What have you tried to do so far to resolve this difficulty? When you are feeling down, what do you do about it? Who knows about this concern of yours? What do you hope that I can do to help you? By using reflective skills that encourage the child to elaborate on what he has presented, you will find that these questions rarely need to be asked directly. Eventually, both you and the child will have a clearer idea of what the child is struggling with, and with which part of the problem he most wants assistance.

Exploration. Once you have identified the "presenting complaint," the next logical step is to dig deeper into what is going on, to discover how this concern is related to the person's life. You will continue to use reflective skills to help him clarify what he is feeling and thinking. Applying the skill of "advanced-level empathy" will help him get at the hidden, disguised, and subtle nuances of his experience. Empathy means that you are able to get inside someone else's skin to the point that you can sense what he or she is going through. In this exploration stage you will use your sensitivity and understanding of the person's experience to help him move to deeper levels of awareness.

The boy without friends might be helped to explore the depth of his feelings of loneliness and estrangement from others. He would become aware of how much he misses having close friends, how much he wishes he could change his situation. With probing from you, he also articulates some of the anger he feels toward his parents for moving him away from his old neighborhood where he had been perfectly content. Prior to this conversation, he had never been able to say out loud how much he still grieved the loss of his old friends and how resentful he still felt for being pulled away without his consent.

Understanding. The deeper the exploration of one's feelings and thoughts, the more profound the insights that are generated as a result of this process. The helper, at this point, uses more active skills such as confrontation, interpretation, self-disclosure, and the giving of information to help the child understand his own role in creating his difficulty. Furthermore, insights are typically generated around understanding why and how the problem developed, what the child is doing to sabotage himself from improving, and what themes are being repeated over and over in his life.

The lonely child is confronted with the realization that his prior life was not as wonderful as he makes it out to be. In fact, he was also lonely in his old neighborhood; the only reason it seemed like he had more friends was because there were more children around the immediate vicinity of his home. He still had not been close to many others. He, therefore, began to accept more responsibility for his own plight. He looked at his fears of being rejected and his strategies of scaring other people away before they had the chance to reject him. He also learned about the self-defeating ways in which he stopped himself from initiating more relationships: He would tell himself negative things and exaggerate the consequences of what could go wrong if somebody did not want to play with him. Finally, he realized that he did have the power to change this whole pattern of his life if only he were willing to take some risks and try some new ways of acting.

Action. Although understanding and insight are wonderful things, without action to change one's behavior they are virtually useless. There are many people walking around this earth who understand, with perfect clarity, why they are so messed up, but they refuse to do anything to change their ways. The action stage of helping is thus geared to helping children translate what they know and understand into a plan that will get them what they want.

The first part of this action process involves establishing goals that the child wishes to reach. Next, using a variety of skills ranging from problem solving to role-playing, the teacher helps the child generate a list of viable alternative courses of action, to narrow them down to those that seem most realistic and attractive, and then to make a commitment to follow through on one's intentions.

The lonely boy is helped to clarify exactly what he would like to be able to do that he is unable or unwilling to do, most notably, (a) initiate new relationships, (b) overcome his fears of rejection, and (c) stop doing things that tend to drive people away. He is helped to define more specifically what these goals mean, in other words, to break down in smaller steps what it means to initiate relationships or what specific things he is prone to doing that turn people off. He is then helped to digest small, bite-size pieces of his ultimate goal, slowly making incremental progress. He might start out initiating a pleasant exchange with someone in his class or sharing his dessert during lunch, for example.

From there, he might eventually work up to asking someone new if he could join him or her for lunch. After practicing these realistic tasks that he would assign to himself, he would be able to invite someone over to his house to play, and more important, not be devastated if the child could not or would not come.

Evaluation. The final stage in the helping process involves evaluating with the person the extent to which he or she has reached desired goals. This systematic assessment of progress helps you measure the impact of your interventions and helps the other person take inventory of what has been accomplished as well as what is left to do.

Because as a principal there are limits to the time and opportunities you have to guide a child all the way through this process, referral will play an important part in your helping effort. If you can do nothing else, you want children and adults to have had a good experience talking to you so that they will be more inclined to take your direction when you urge them to seek additional help.

One frustrated parent, for example, did make considerable progress in overcoming her reluctance to be more assertive in dealing with her son's teacher. More important, the principal helped her to clarify her feelings about her plight and recognize that her dissatisfaction with the teacher-parent relationship had as much to do with her behavior as with the teacher's.

In addition to her communication difficulties with the teacher, the parent also suffered from low self-esteem due in part to the constant verbal and physical abuse she received from her spouse. Because of these complications, the principal soon realized that she neither had the expertise nor the responsibility to work on this problem. She therefore decided in her evaluative process to recommend that the mother seek help from an agency that specifically dealt with such issues. Recognizing your limitations in both time and specialized counseling skills will help you know when to refer.

The Link Between the Counseling Process and Helping Skills

Now that you have an understanding of the "big picture" of functioning in a counseling role with both children and adults, you can appreciate that you will need a number of skills to capitalize on therapeutic elements and to move through the sequential stages of helping. Although we have mentioned that certain skills, such as questioning and reflecting, are usually linked to the assessment and exploration stages, in reality you will use almost all of the different counselor behaviors in all phases of your helping efforts.

Suggested Activities

1. Define how a professional helping relationship is different from a relationship with friends.
2. Think of an unresolved issue in your life. Apply the steps of the counseling process to work yourself through (a) an assessment of the issue, (b) an understanding of the underlying themes and connected issues, (c) an action plan of what you propose to do, and (d) how you intend to evaluate the results of your effort.
3. Being nonjudgmental and accepting are important elements in the helping process. Identify several subjects that may come up in conversations with children, parents, and teachers about which you feel very strongly (abortion, drug use, sexual

activity, discrimination, etc.). Imagine someone expresses values that are the antithesis of your own. Formulate responses that would avoid imposing a critical, judgmental attitude.

Suggested Readings

Corey, G. (1999). *Theory and practice of counseling and psychotherapy* (6th ed.). Pacific Grove, CA: Brooks/Cole.

Gazda, G. M. (1995). *Human relations development: A manual for educators.* Boston: Allyn & Bacon.

Kottler, J. A. (1993). *On being a therapist.* San Francisco: Jossey-Bass.

McEwan, E. K. (1996). *"Nobody likes me." Helping your child make friends.* Wheaton, IL: Harold Shaw.

Meier, S. T., & Davis, S. T. (1993). *The elements of counseling* (2nd ed.). Pacific Grove, CA: Brooks/Cole.

Sommers-Flanagan, J., & Sommers-Flanagan, R. (1997). *Tough kids, cool counseling: User-friendly approaches with challenging youth.* Alexandria, VA: American Counseling Association.

4

——■——

Developing Skills of Helping

A lthough the focus of our discussion now turns to the skills of relating to all the members of your school family in a helpful capacity, much of your success in these endeavors will depend on things you do inside your own head before the conversation even starts. Counseling encounters, you see, are different from normal human interactions because of the helper's state of mind as he or she enters the relationships. Counseling is, in a way, a form of meditation in which both participants are concentrating intently on what the other is saying; it is as if nothing or nobody else exists outside the circle of their interaction.

Counselors and therapists are often accused of being able to read minds when, in fact, what they are doing is simply focusing all their attention and energy, their very being, on what the other person is saying, doing, and meaning by the person's words or gestures. With such full and complete attention toward others, it is indeed possible to anticipate what they will say next and even what they are thinking, even though they haven't fully articulated these ideas to themselves.

Before you begin a counseling encounter, it is thus extremely important to take steps to clear your mind of all distractions, to put aside your own worries, your grumbling stomach, and the tasks you must complete later in the day. Removing distractions is particularly difficult in the principalship. Everyone wants a "piece" of the principal and if you thrive on this high-energy, ever-changing environment, slowing down to listen will take discipline.

In yoga, meditation, martial arts, or any contemplative art (of which counseling is certainly a part), participants are encouraged to take a "cleansing breath" before they begin their activity. A deep breath helps clear yourself of muddled and distracting thoughts and helps "center" yourself on the interaction that is about to begin. This breath comes to symbolize the commitment that you are making to the individual, that for the next few minutes nothing exists except your interest and caring for him or her. If you experiment with this kind of attitude in other relationships in your life, you will notice a remarkable change taking place in the quality and intimacy of your interactions.

Once you have cleared your mind and focused your concentration, it is then imperative that you monitor your internal attitudes. Counselors are helpful precisely because they are perceived as being nonjudgmental, accepting, and noncritical. Whereas outside the helping encounter you could quite easily feel critical toward what you are hearing, once you have made a decision to function in a helping role, you are making a decision to suspend, temporarily, that part of you that judges others; judgments interfere with your ability to respond compassionately to what you are hearing. If someone senses even a little bit of authoritarian criticism on your part, all trust can be lost.

In this initial stage of making contact, before you even open your mouth to say anything or apply your first helping skill, you are already setting in motion an internal state of mind, a set of helping attitudes, to help yourself be maximally receptive and responsive to what you will hear. You are reminding yourself to stay flexible, to push aside distractions, and to feel compassionate toward what is about to take place.

Attending

Easier than it may sound, appearing attentive to your students, staff, or parents is the first and most basic task in being helpful. If you would simply monitor yourself and others during most interactions, you would notice how rare it is that people are being fully attentive to one another. While addressing you, and purportedly listening, a friend is also probably engaged in a number of simultaneous activities—looking over your shoulder, waving to someone walking by, rustling through papers, grooming hair. Such divided behavior hardly inspires your confidence, nor does it communicate that you are all that important to that person during that moment in time.

Attending to someone means giving them your total, complete, undivided interest. It means using your body, your face, your eyes,

yes, especially your eyes, to say, "Nothing exists right now for me except you. Every ounce of my energy and being is focused on you." This calls for structuring any one-on-one time with an individual in an atmosphere that is free from interruptions. Move to a round table where you can sit side by side (or face to face) with the child or adult. Clear away any clutter. Remove anything that might distract you from complete concentration. Turn off the telephones.

You would be truly amazed at how healing this simple act can be—giving another person your full attention. Children, in particular, are often so used to being devalued by adults that attending behaviors instantly tell them something is different about this interaction: "Here is a person who seems to care about me and what I have to say." But even adults in today's fast-track world will find having the full attention of an "important" person like the principal a somewhat rare and enormously affirming experience.

Listening

Attending skills involve the use of nonverbal behaviors (head nods, smiles, eye contact, body positions) and minimal verbal encouragement ("uh-huh," "I see") to communicate your intense interest in what a person is saying. Although these skills are a requirement to earn a person's trust, they are relatively empty gestures unless you are actually listening and can prove that you have understood.

This presents an interesting challenge: How do you demonstrate to people that you understand them? How do you show them that you not only heard what they said, but you really know what they mean?

There are two ways to show evidence of such synchronized attention: passive listening, which we have already described in the context of nonverbal and verbal attending, and active listening, in which you take a more direct role in responding to what you heard. Ultimately, listening is communicated by the way you respond to the speaker, by your ability to prove that you really did hear what has been said.

Empathic Resonance

Empathy is the ability (and willingness) to crawl inside someone else's skin and to know what he or she is experiencing, to "walk a mile in another's moccasins." This is where attending, listening, and interpersonal sensitivity come together in such a way that you are able to get outside yourself enough so that you can sense what the other person is feeling and thinking. The second part of this helping behavior involves communicating your understanding of what you hear/see/sense/feel in such a way that the student, staff member, or parent does not feel quite so alone. At its most basic level, beginning counselors are taught to use the stem "You feel ____" to respond to each client statement. Although this may sound artificial and contrived, it does help to get one in the habit of focusing on and resonating with an individual's "felt experience."

Let's put together these first three skills into a dialogue with a teacher who is upset about a poor summative evaluation:

Teacher: I can't believe what you wrote about me in my evaluation. (Said accusingly, with tears in her eyes.)

Principal: (Puts down report she was reading. Steps to her office door to gently close it and moves from her desk to a round conference table. Turns her chair to face the teacher fully. Softens her face and waits patiently [attending].) Yes, that's true. You did receive some unacceptable ratings. [Note the way the statement is reworded—placing emphasis on teacher's responsibility.]

Teacher: Well, I don't think you're right! The evaluation is too picky.

Principal: (Nods head [attending].) You don't think the evaluation deals with behaviors and attitudes that are important for a teacher to exhibit. [Active listening.]

Teacher: Well, yes. And I know I'm not perfect, but this evaluation is going to ruin my chances for getting on the career ladder.

Principal: You're really feeling disappointed, and even angry, about the result. [Reflection of feeling.]

Teacher: Everybody's going to hear about these ratings, and I'll be embarrassed in front of the whole staff.

Principal: (Nods her head [attending]. Smiles reassuringly [passive listening].) Yes, I can see how difficult this is for you. You are really feeling under a lot of pressure. [Empathic resonance.] Let's explore some ways we can take the pressure off and still help you achieve your career ladder goal.

As is evident from this helping encounter, these first counseling skills are connected to one another in that they all attempt to build an open, trusting, and accepting atmosphere in which the teacher will feel comfortable disclosing and exploring her feelings.

Exploration Skills

Questioning

Certainly, the most obvious and direct way to gather information or encourage individuals to explore a particular area is to ask them a series of questions. As you read the previous dialogue, probably a number of ideas came to mind: Why do you feel the evaluation was unfair? Have you taken the time to pat yourself on the back for the "good news" in the evaluation? Can you think of any things you could do to change the unsatisfactory ratings to satisfactory?

The problem with questions, as natural as they may come to mind, is that they often put another individual in a "one down" position in which you are the interrogator and expert problem solver. "Tell me what the situation is and I will fix it." For that reason, questions are used only when you can't get the individual to reveal information in other ways. You would be amazed at how much territory you can cover by relying on other, more indirect methods of exploration.

If you must ask questions, word them in such a way that they are *open-ended*, or the kind that can't be answered with a single word, rather than *close-ended*, those that can be satisfied with a one-word response.

Contrast the differences in the examples below:

Close-ended	*Open-ended*
Are you feeling upset right now?	What are you feeling?
Would you like me to tell you why?	What can I offer you right now?
Are you going to change some of your ineffective teaching practices?	What are you going to do?

It is fairly obvious that open-ended questions encourage further exploration, whereas close-ended queries tend to cut off communication. You may have the answer to your question but at the expense of prolonged silence in which the teacher or student is waiting for you to continue directing the course of the conversation.

One notable exception to the rule of avoiding questions whenever possible, especially close-ended ones, is when it is important to gather very specific information in a potentially threatening or dangerous situation. If an individual, for example, expressed suicidal fantasies, it would in that case be very appropriate to ask specific questions: "Have you ever tried it before? Do you have a plan for how you would do it? Do you have the means to carry out your plan? Will you promise me not to do anything at all until we can get you some help?" A yes response to the first three questions and no to the last would signal the need to take some definite preventive action beyond the scope of merely reflecting the individual's feelings.

Reflecting Content

An indirect way to help someone further explore his or her concerns is to use your listening and empathy skills to reflect the content of what he or she is saying. This does not mean you should sound like a parrot, but rather it indicates that by rewording you have heard accurately what was said. These restatements help people to clarify further what they are saying and facilitate additional exploration into the issues.

Child: Mikey keeps hitting me. He won't leave me alone and teases me all of the time.

Principal: Mikey won't get off your back no matter what you do.

In this simple reflection of content, the principal acknowledges what was heard and also guides the focus toward the child's own behavior ("no matter what you do").

Reflecting Feelings

This skill is quite similar to the previous one but has a different emphasis: on feelings rather than content. The intent here is to identify and reflect the underlying emotions that you hear expressed in a person's statements. Although this may, at first, seem like an easy thing to do, it is among the most complex and difficult tasks that counselors undertake. To reflect feelings sensitively, accurately, and helpfully, you must to be able to (a) listen very carefully to subtle nuances of what is being said, (b) decode the deeper meanings of communication, (c) identify accurately the feelings a person is experiencing, and (d) communicate this understanding in a way that it can be accepted.

Child: My mom thinks I should talk to you about something bad that's gonna happen, but I'm not sure.

Principal: You're feeling some pressure from your friends, but you still need to talk about something that's bothering you. [Note the first part reflects the content, the second part identifies the apprehension.]

Child: Yeah, I do need to talk about this, I guess. (Silence.)

Principal: It's hard for you to do this. [Even silence can be reflected.]

Child: (Deep breath.) Here goes. Some of my friends are planning to break into the school this weekend and steal some computers. If I don't go along with their plan they're really going to be mad at me.

Principal: You're in a real jam where it seems like whatever you do, you're going to end up in trouble with someone. You're really confused about whether to listen to your friends, your parents, or yourself.

Child: Yeah, I can't sleep so good just worrying about it. I like the computer teacher and I couldn't do something like that to him.

Principal: But you feel loyalty to your friends too.

Child: Yeah. What's more important? Loyalty or honesty?

And so continues a dialogue in which the principal relies on reflection of feeling and content to help the child explore the issues, to help him clarify what he really wants, and eventually to help him resolve what he wants to do—to make his own decision—apart from pressures from his peers. It is through such an exchange that it is possible for children, as well as adults, to find out what they truly believe in and act on those convictions.

Self-Disclosure

This is the skill in which you demonstrate authenticity, genuineness, and humanness to the children and adults in your school. Idealizing us as they sometimes do, it may be helpful for them to hear the ways that we have struggled with similar issues (if that is the case) and to connect with us on an intimate level.

Because this intervention has the potential for abuse (talking about yourself too much, too often, at inappropriate times, or revealing inappropriate material), self-disclosure should be concise, devoid of self-indulgence, and used very conservatively. The danger is that by revealing too much about yourself, you will violate professional boundaries, reveal information about yourself that could be damaging, or focus too much on yourself.

Self-disclosures are best when you are showing an individual that he or she is not alone, bridging perceived distance between you, and modeling openness.

Principal: I know what you are going through. My parents were divorced when I was your age and I struggled for quite a while before I got my feet back on the ground.

Another variety of self-disclosure, called *immediacy*, involves sharing what you are feeling about the interaction or what you are feeling toward the person at a particular moment in time:

Principal: I'm honored that you've chosen to trust me. I feel closer to you after what you've told me. And I respect you for your courage in dealing with a very tough situation.

Summarizing

Used at least once at the end of any conversation, but which can be inserted any time a wrap-up is needed, the summary ties together themes that were discussed and puts things in perspective. Ideally, you can summarize after having asked the individual to do so first: "So, what are you leaving with?" You can then fill in the gaps.

Principal: Let's summarize what we've talked about so far. You've talked a lot about feeling torn between your friends and your own convictions. You seem to know what you really want to do; that's why you confided in me in the first place. This problem you have is related to others in the past you've experienced—when you follow along with others rather than listening to your conscience.

What else did I leave out that you'd like to add?

A good summary logically provides a transition between the exploration phase of helping and the action strategies for making needed changes.

Action Skills

Principals are often called on to "leap tall buildings in a single bound," but your role will limit the action strategies you can employ for individuals with whom you counsel. This will be frustrating for you because the one thing you will want to do—and that all beginners try to do—is to jump in and fix the problem, or at least fix what you think is the problem. Most often, your helping role will be to listen, to understand, to communicate empathy as you're helping the person to clarify what the issues are. Then, if needed, you will refer the individual to other staff members for appropriate professional help.

At times, however, you will have the opportunity to help the individual convert what has been discussed into some constructive action. The following skills are thus described to you with a note of caution: Get more training and supervision before you attempt any intrusive means of intervention. That especially includes giving advice, the single most abused helping strategy.

Advice Giving

Don't do it. Period. Resist your natural inclination to tell people what to do with their lives. Are you sure you know what is best for anyone else? Do you really know what is best for you? Are you sure you want the responsibility that comes with telling someone else what to do?

The exceptions to this prohibition take place only when children are tempted to do something that is potentially dangerous to themselves or others. Then you are not only permitted but required to do something.

Remember, however, that the way you offer advice will determine the extent to which a child is likely to pay attention and follow your words of wisdom.

Principal: I think that before you take such a drastic step, you should talk to some other people first. Tell your friends, only the ones you trust, what you have in mind. Hear what they have to say. Then let's talk again.

Goal Setting

This is the consummate action skill, the one that satisfies the needs of both participants in the counseling process to translate some elusive, ambiguous issue into concrete results. Unlike dreaded homework assignments, however, this kind of goal is definitely not prescribed by you—many individuals already may feel resentment toward anyone in authority for telling them what to do. Instead, you will take the longer, more laborious route of helping them define and follow through on their own stated goals—that way, they are much more likely to complete them. And even if they don't do what they said they would, you can unconcernedly shrug and say, "Oh, well, I guess you didn't want to do it after all." Then, when the individual replies, "But I did! I did want to do it. I just didn't have time," you can smile and reply, "Fine. You'll do it when you want."

There are other factors to keep in mind when helping people to set goals for themselves:

1. *Make sure the goal they identify is really related to the central issue they are struggling with.* Losing 10 pounds may be a very good thing to do, but if one's weight isn't the major impediment to high self-esteem, then efforts could be wasted.

2. *Construct goals that are realistic and attainable.* A staff member enthusiastic to change can become overzealous, naively believing he can do everything overnight. Help people take small, manageable steps, ensuring they will experience success in their efforts. A child

who has few friends, for example, could start with carrying on 2-minute-long conversations with others before undertaking progressively more difficult tasks.

3. *Whenever possible, make the goals as specific as possible.* Include what the person will do, where he or she will do it, when and how often it will be done, for how long it will be continued, with whom, who will be present, and what contingencies will be in place if he or she should falter. These factors can help translate a person's imprecise concerns into action goals.

For example:

Before: I get in fights a lot. I want to stop but other kids sometimes push me too far. I let them do that. I also know that I can't keep fighting all the time or I won't have any friends left. No teeth either. So, I guess what I have to do is stop fighting so much.

After: Between now and tomorrow at this time I will not get in a single physical fight with anyone at school. (I can't guarantee what might happen at home with my brothers.) If I should start to lose my temper during the next day at school, I will repeat to myself what we've talked about. If that doesn't work too well, I give you my word, no, I mean I promise to myself that I will walk away. If I absolutely have to defend myself I will only do so with my mouth, not my fists.

As can be seen, this young man's goal for the next 24 hours meets the criteria described earlier. Sometimes, you can make a tremendous difference in people's lives by having them talk things out and decide what they want to do, then help them to create a plan for how they can get what they want.

Problem Solving

A more elaborate version of goal setting, involving a sequential series of steps, is applying a problem-solving approach to an individual's difficulties. Assume, for example, that a parent wants to develop a more consistent discipline plan at home. She feels frustrated and hopeless, ready to throw in the towel and send the kids to their dad. Any problem-solving strategy would (a) help define the problem, (b) specify the goals, (c) develop alternatives that might be constructive, (d) narrow the choices to those that seem most realistic, and (e) put the plan into action.

With the help of the principal, the parent generated a list of unacceptable behaviors, suggested several ways in which she could change her own behavior, and selected one goal for her and the children to work on during the next 2 weeks.

Reframing

Imagine a well-painted landscape in an ugly frame, one that so detracts from the art that it loses its luster and appeal. Take the same painting, put it in a different frame, and voilà!—a thing of true beauty! Using a well-chosen and more appropriate frame to set off the true beauty of a work of art is analogous to reframing in a helping context.

Reframing, although a creative and challenging endeavor, is a skill that is difficult to learn. It is a way of thinking about things that people present to you in a completely different light. Your task is to take a problem that someone describes, usually one that you can do absolutely nothing about, and then reframe it in such a way that solutions more readily suggest themselves. In its most basic mode, you take what the student (or adult) has said—"I'm stupid" (a predicament that if it were true, you could do little to help)—and then alter it in such a way that it appears more easily resolvable: "You are less talented than you would like to be in math, but you are quite brilliant at drawing funny pictures and fixing things that are broken. That doesn't sound like someone who is stupid to me."

Some other examples of reframing in action are the following:

Statement	Reframing
"I'm shy."	"You act shyly when you are in new situations without your close friends around."
"I hate school."	"You don't enjoy structured learning very much, but you really do like school when you have freedom to do what you want."

"The teachers accuse my child of being disruptive and I know he isn't."	"Your child has a great sense of humor. He is just performing for the wrong audience."
"The teacher is boring."	"It's hard for you to concentrate on content presentations."

In each case, the principal seeks to reframe the definition of the problem in a more optimistic light. Sometimes this works, sometimes it doesn't. As with all helping efforts, we try a variety of approaches until we find the right combination.

Cognitive Restructuring

Reframing is a cognitive intervention that helps people shift the way they view their concerns. Other techniques help individuals think differently about their plights, the most popular of which are known as rational-emotive therapy developed by Albert Ellis and cognitive therapy developed by Aaron Beck. The theory behind these techniques is quite simple: What we feel is based on how we think about what is happening. If we change the way we interpret a predicament, we can thus change how we feel about it. Our job, then, is to teach people to realize they have choices about how they can react to events in their lives. Very little is intrinsically bad or annoying or frustrating. It is our perception of these experiences that determine our reactions. "If you don't like how you are feeling," the cognitive therapist says, "then change how you feel about it!"

This approach to helping should be exciting to you for a number of reasons. First, it is easily learned, and with a little practice you will find yourself becoming more and more skilled at helping people understand that the way they think about their problems determines, to a great extent, how they subsequently feel and behave. Second, this is a problem-solving approach that you can apply immediately to your own life. In fact, the more you work on your own internal thinking patterns, the more proficient you will be in helping others with theirs. Likewise, the more you practice helping others confront their irrational beliefs and illogical thoughts, the more you will notice profound changes in your own personal effectiveness. Third, and most exciting of all, using these cognitive strategies can make a difference in an individual's life in a very short period of time.

The process of cognitive helping follows a fairly logical sequence in which you first help an individual to articulate the feelings that are bothersome. The helping skills mentioned earlier (active listening, reflections of feeling, open-ended questioning) are often useful.

Principal: How are you feeling about your new assignment at the new school?

Teacher: I don't know. I'm not really crazy about the idea, I guess. But what choice do I have?

Principal: You seem pretty upset about the way this was handled.

Teacher: Damn right I am! Why did I have to be one to get shifted around?

Principal: It seems so unfair.

Teacher: I'm going to be leaving my support group of friends here and I'll have a much longer commute. My whole life will be turned upside down.

The teacher is feeling that her life will be ruined because she won't be teaching in the same location next year. She has lost control of her life and will be forced to recreate a new circle of friends.

So far, the principal has helped the teacher identify four different feelings she is experiencing: upset, depression, anger, and hurt. With more time, the list could be lengthened even further because we usually feel many different things when we are upset about something.

Next, the teacher would be encouraged to describe the particular situation that she believes is causing her the problems. At this juncture, the teacher describes exactly what took place.

Principal: Why do you suppose this transfer was arranged in the first place?

Teacher: Well, I have certification in middle school language arts, and they need another teacher in that area.

Principal: So, you're one of the few teachers qualified for the position.

Teacher: Well, yes. But I can also coach cheerleading. I was the captain of my cheerleading squad in college.

Because the point of this helping procedure is that other people or events don't make you feel anything—you make yourself feel things based on how you think—the next step is to help the teacher identify the internal thoughts or irrational beliefs that are creating the suffering. This part is a bit tricky because it requires you to be familiar with the main themes prevalent in irrational thinking. Basically, irrational beliefs fall into three main groups.

First, *exaggerating reality* makes things seem much worse than they really are by distorting the significance of what took place: "Because I have to teach in a different location, my life is ruined." "It's terrible that I will be relocated like this." It may be inconvenient, uncomfortable, undesirable, or unwelcome that certain things happen in life, but words like *terrible* and *awful* imply that a true disaster has occurred rather than a mere setback. This may sound like it's quibbling with a few words, but language determines a lot about how we perceive things and what we subsequently feel.

Second, *demanding that the world be different* results from expectations that the world or people be different than they are. We set ourselves up as special beings who deserve special attention. Common manifestations of this irrational thinking usually begin with the pronouncement: "It's not fair . . .

　. . . that I didn't get what I want."
　. . . that he treated me that way."
　. . . that the rules were changed."
　. . . that I was involuntarily transferred."

This thinking is irrational because, clearly, the world is not fair. We are not entitled to special attention. And just because we have certain expectations for people, it does not mean they are obligated to live up to them.

"While it might not be preferred that you are transferred to this school, that's the way the system works for everyone. If the world was truly a fair place, you would get what you want and what you deserve. This is just one of those times when you have to make the best of things. You can't alter the transfer but you can choose how you're going to live with it."

Third, *judging oneself in absolute terms* is a variation of the previous irrational thinking in which you apply unrealistic or perfectionistic standards to yourself that you could never live up to.

For example:

"Because I didn't perform as well as I would like in this situation, I will never be good at this, or anything."

"Because I got a D on this exam, I am stupid."

"Because my child has been diagnosed with a learning disability, I'm a failure as a parent."

"Because I'm being transferred, I must be a failure."

Words like *must*, *should*, and *never* are cues we are making demands of ourselves that are self-imposed and probably not realistic.

Even with this thumbnail sketch of irrational themes, you have some idea of how the principal could move an individual to the last and most important stage: challenging those irrational beliefs and confronting their veracity.

These interventions require that you are able to apply cognitive techniques to yourself before you can work successfully with others. In other words, you can't talk people into letting go of their dysfunctional thinking unless you can dispute your own.

In the case we have been following, the dialogue might develop as follows:

Principal: So what you are saying is that because you're being transferred, your life is ruined.

Teacher: That's about it. I won't even be able to enjoy teaching anymore.

Principal: It's impossible for you to enjoy teaching anywhere else but here.

Teacher: But I started my teaching career here and I always envisioned myself in the same place.

Principal: I understand that. The part that makes no sense is that you are saying that because you have enjoyed a wonderful experience teaching here and are now being asked to teach in some other place because of your expertise, that you won't be able to enjoy the profession you love anymore.

Teacher: OK. So maybe I exaggerated a little. But you have to agree that the whole transfer process is ridiculous. Only the teachers who aren't politically connected have to inconvenience their whole lives.

Principal: Let's assume that you are right: It wasn't fair. So what?

Teacher: Huh?

Principal: Since when is life fair and impartial?

Teacher: But it should be fair! I mean . . .

Principal: That's not the point. Look, you can't change what happened. There's a contract and the administration is abiding by it. But you can change the way you think about it. The only thing worse than not being able to stay here in your comfort zone is not having a job at all.

This interaction gives you a flavor of the rich opportunities available to teach adults and children alike to feel more control over their internal states. Many individuals feel so little power in their lives that it is especially exciting to introduce them to a way of thinking that allows them to decide how they want to feel about things.

The "map" in Table 4.1 highlights the strategy in which individuals are challenged to

1. Accept greater responsibility for their thoughts and feelings.
2. Be more aware of what is going on inside their heads.
3. Become more analytical and logical in the ways they reason through cause-effect relationships.
4. Make choices about how they want to react to the things and people around them.
5. Change the ways they feel by altering the ways they think.

The principal closes her talk with the teacher by reinforcing these very ideas:

Principal: It is no wonder you were upset. It wasn't only a matter of being transferred but also the way you reacted to that situation. It is understandable that you would be disappointed, but not so down that you can barely function—that you did to yourself. Any time in the future you don't like the way you are feel-

TABLE 4.1 Map of Cognitive Interventions

A	B	C	D
	Irrational Beliefs	Emotional Consequence	Disputing Irrational Beliefs
The Incident			
"I was transferred against my will."	1. "My career is ruined."	Anger	1. "Your career is changed, not ruined."
	2. "I'll never survive this."	Frustration	2. "You will not only survive this, you could even choose to flourish."
	3. "It's not fair that I've been treated this way."	Depression	3. "You're right, it's not fair. So what?"
	4. "This means I've somehow failed."	Shame	4. "This may be only a minor setback."
	5. "This is awful!"	Hopelessness	5. "This is not a catastrophe, only an annoyance."

ing, you can follow this same procedure of figuring out what you are saying to yourself about the event and then change your internal thoughts.

The object of these confrontations is to help a person realize the extent of his or her distortions and substitute more realistic and appropriate responses. Confrontations come in other forms as well. The whole process we just went through is reviewed in Table 4.1.

In stressful or upsetting situations, the goal is not to eliminate all emotions but merely to reduce those that are out of control or undesirable. In this case, it isn't realistic for the teacher to feel nothing at all but rather to feel more moderate levels of distress given the circumstances. After going through this process, the teacher is still upset but not nearly as distressed as before. She no longer feels much anger at all. In some ways, she has even been helped to "reframe" the situation as a new challenge for her to tackle.

Confrontations

There are times when people need to hear they have crossed a boundary or when they need to understand the discrepancies between what they are doing and what they said they want, or what they are saying now versus what they said earlier. The secret is to confront someone in such a way that he or she will not feel defensive. The best confrontations are thus presented neutrally, matter-of-factly, even tentatively, as if to say that you have noticed something interesting that they might find helpful: "I'm confused. You are saying that you want to apply for the career ladder program but you show no evidence of improving your classroom management."

Or to a parent: "You say you're concerned about your daughter's progress in school, but you've canceled the last three conferences we've scheduled."

You are putting the observation before individuals and letting them decide what they want to do about it. This is, obviously, the most intrusive of interventions and, hence, the one that must be applied most cautiously and carefully. You can as easily alienate or wound someone deeply with a mistimed or insensitive confrontation as you can help facilitate a major breakthrough. The key, therefore, before attempting any confrontation, is to ask yourself whether you are offering this intervention out of caring for the other person or whether it represents an attempt to be punitive or to put the person down.

Encouragement

We saved the best for last. Many students and teachers will experience certain concerns for which there are no easy solutions and that you can do little about except offer support. Encouragement is listed here as an action skill because it is a deliberate and intentional effort on your part to foster hope in those who are without it.

Imagine a parent who finds out her child has leukemia, a child whose father died in a hunting accident, or a staff member who has just suffered her third miscarriage. What would you propose to do in these situations? The answer, of course, is that your act of doing is really one of encouragement. You communicate, in effect, that you have complete confidence that the individual will indeed recover a positive state of mind. Furthermore, you intend to be there for him or her along the way. Because you believe in the person's power and strength, he or she will regain a sense of balance. Sometimes, your support is all that you have to give.

Suggested Activities

1. Find a partner to work with and practice the skills mentioned in this chapter. Start with basic attending skills:
   a. Carry on a conversation with your partner in which neither of you maintains eye contact; then, after a few minutes, concentrate on making good eye contact; notice the difference.
   b. Continue your conversation but with both of you showing blank expressions on your faces; after a few minutes, both of you show animation, warmth, and expressiveness in your face; notice the difference.
   c. As you continue your talk, add to these attending skills a more concerted effort on your part to use head nods, "uh-huhs," and other acknowledgments that you are following and understanding what your partner is saying; notice the effect.

2. Choose a partner to work with. One of you decide to be the "client" first while the other of you will be the "helper." The client should play the role of a child who feels left out of activities during recess and wants to stay inside. The helper should only respond with active listening skills, primarily restatements and reflections of feeling.

3. With a partner, you can practice asking open-ended questions that encourage rather than cut off communication. Each of you write down three questions that you believe will elicit

maximum information from your partner and encourage him or her to examine important issues. Ask your questions of one another and note their effectiveness.

4. Concentrate on a few of the skills presented in this chapter and make them part of the normal way you relate to others. Find opportunities every day in which you can practice your new skills.

5. Recruit the assistance of an expert who can observe you applying the skills in this chapter (or record an interview on tape). Ask for specific feedback on ways you could improve your performance.

6. Select an incident in your life about which you feel some lingering distress. Apply the cognitive intervention strategy presented in this chapter to help yourself:
   a. Label what you are feeling.
   b. Identify the irrational beliefs and distorted interpretations that are creating your suffering.
   c. Dispute the irrational beliefs.
   d. Write down each stage of the process.

Make a commitment to incorporate this way of processing emotional discomfort into your life by practicing several times each day.

Suggested Readings

Cormier, W. H., & Cormier, L. S. (1998). *Interviewing strategies for helpers* (4th ed.). Pacific Grove, CA: Brooks/Cole.

Egan, G. (1998). *The skilled helper* (6th ed.). Pacific Grove, CA: Brooks/Cole.

Evans, D. R., Hearn, M. T., Uhlemann, M. R., & Ivey, A. E. (1997). *Essential interviewing: A programmed approach to effective communication* (4th ed.). Pacific Grove, CA: Brooks/Cole.

Sklare, G. (1997). *Brief counseling that works: A solution-focused approach for school counselors.* Thousand Oaks, CA: Corwin.

5

Helping Strategies in Groups

You can apply the skills of helping in settings other than individual conferences. Although there is no substitute for the intimacy and focused attention of being with an individual in private, the goals that can be accomplished in groups have the power to unify, empower, and energize all the group members. Working with children, parents, and teachers in groups is an alternative way to help many people deal with troublesome issues like playground conflicts, lack of motivation, or social skills. Working with staff and/or parents in groups can involve a wide range of possibilities to include building and sharing values, developing effective teams, generating ideas, sharing critical information, problem solving, reaching consensus, resolving conflict, planning, and goal setting.

Critical Attributes of Process Groups

Your administrative education may not have included training in group dynamics or group process. Consequently, you may be ill at ease when faced with the prospect of an entire afternoon of "released time" in which to work on team building or develop an improvement plan. You may feel intimidated by the variety of personalities and agendas represented in your faculty. You may find conflict and heated discussion hard to handle.

Although you were once a classroom teacher, you may even feel awkward about working with an entire classroom to process the death of their teacher or the injury of one of their classmates. These feelings are natural and understandable. But you can become more confident about helping groups. Developing the skills to work with small and large groups is an important aspect of instructional leadership and will affect your ability to realize your vision for your school.

If the idea of "process" groups is new to you, you are about to add some exciting new strategies to your administrative repertoire. A process is an activity or structure that can help facilitate the various types of group goals we mentioned above. You, as the group leader, will become a process expert, rather than being the expert with all of the answers. As a process expert with students, you may help a group to resolve a conflict, learn a social skill, or solve a classroom or schoolwide problem. As a process expert with adults, you may (a) help your student, staff, or parent group to ask the right questions; (b) help them to discuss and debate ideas openly and freely; (c) help to create a climate in which they can make judgments and choices; and (d) help them commit to the implementation of their choices.

Process-Oriented Groups for Children

Process-oriented groups provide different kinds of educational experiences for children. Specifically, these growth-oriented experiences differ from the usual classroom instruction in the following ways:

1. *The emphasis is not on content.* There is no specific information that you wish students to learn in process groups. Your intent, instead, is to provide a safe environment in which children may explore their own values, feelings, and beliefs about themselves, about others, and about their experiences.

2. *Participants are encouraged to share their own personal reactions to ideas rather than ideas themselves.* Unlike the usual classroom activities that focus on intellectual ideas or the development of skills, process groups require participants to speak about their very personal reactions to what they have experienced and are experiencing.

3. *Small talk, rambling, and focus on outsiders is not permitted.* It is crucial to keep attention on what is taking place in the group. You do not let children complain about what others are doing, nor do you

let them ramble, intellectualize, or engage in meaningless prattle; you keep them focused on what they are feeling and thinking. You make sure that time is equitably distributed among all children.

4. *Process groups are student centered rather than leader centered.* In process groups, the leader plays a supportive role—it is the children who do most of the talking and are clearly the ones whose contributions are most important. The leader's role is not to instruct but rather to guide the process.

5. *Children speak only for themselves.* The pronoun *I* is emphasized over *we* or *you*. The object is to help students to express themselves more honestly, to clarify their own beliefs, and to respond to one another sensitively.

6. *The leader's attention is focused primarily on the dynamics and process of the group.* It is not so much what the children say as how they say it, and their relationship to one another, that draws the leader's attention. Who is getting along with whom? What coalitions have formed? What degree of cohesion has developed? What do the children avoid talking about? What is the meaning of any silence?

Principals must take caution and care in their personal structuring of process groups. Not only are you delving into a domain outside of your traditional expertise, but many parents are threatened by any attempt to intrude into their private lives. Furthermore, they believe that parents bear the ultimate responsibility and are the primary authority for teaching their own children values, morals, religion, family traditions, socialization, and self-worth.

Balancing the privacy and rights of both children and parents with the vast needs that many children and families bring to school is very difficult, but crucial. We believe that it is unwise to structure any long-term process groups with children unless parental advice and permission have been obtained, and/or you have consulted with your professional staff.

Process-Oriented Groups for Adults

We have all encountered teachers or parents who are suspicious of process-oriented groups. They feel that sitting around and talking is a waste of time. They disdain the "touchy-feely" stuff. Just give these folks the facts and the tasks and they'll get the job done. This approach does have its value for short-term, specific goals that are highly technical in nature. However, whenever commitment, trust, purpose, communication, and involvement are important, group processes will be needed to build and strengthen these qualities. A willingness to put group goals above personal goals (commitment) will not happen unless staff members and/or parents understand and share some crucial beliefs and values. Arriving at that kind of understanding takes group process. The development of feelings of confidence and support on the part of group members for each other (trust) can emerge only when time is taken to work through conflicts and differences in group activities. An understanding of the group's mission (purpose); the ability to handle conflict, decision making, and day-to-day interaction (communication); and partnership and involvement in the group's mission (involvement) take hours and hours of processing.

There are many different ways that a principal can employ process group structures in schools, depending on the climate you wish to create and the particular needs of your staff. Here is a list of some possibilities:

1. Arrange a support group on teaching excellence in which teachers talk about their frustrations, joys, and other feelings related to their work. Rotate the leadership role, with you and/or a counselor acting as cofacilitators and process observers.

2. Conduct staff meetings with attention to process, as well as content. In other words, in addition to hitting the agenda items and business issues, also encourage people to share what they are thinking and feeling. As time permits, validate those disclosures that are most appropriate.

3. Schedule a retreat to work on team-building issues. This can be for an afternoon, a day, or a whole weekend. Consult with counselors or central office personnel to help you plan such a process group with attention to building cohesion and trust among staff.

4. Lead a parent sharing group each month in which you listen actively to various concerns. Set limits on griping and com-

plaining, instead keeping the focus on constructive issues. Demonstrate your caring and concern.

5. Take your office and support staff out for lunch. Structure the conversation around genuine sharing to build morale and a team spirit. Stop trying to fix problems and put out fires and instead just listen and encourage others to do so as well.

Advantages and Disadvantages of Process Groups

Process groups have a number of advantages over individual helping efforts. For example, a crisis in the community could reveal that a number of children have concerns about a similar issue (drugs, violence, disasters, etc.). In groups you can obviously reach more children and make more efficient use of your time. Additionally, group structures provide a support system for change, teach children skills for succeeding in social situations, facilitate an atmosphere of intimacy and trust, and most important, provide opportunities for constructive feedback from their peers.

Process groups for the adults with whom you work have the power to empower and motivate. The synergy of group process can energize and renew a "burned out" or "mature" faculty if handled skillfully. Process groups have the power to help a fragmented and fractured parent organization refocus and revitalize its efforts. Process groups are not without their disadvantages, however. Because they can be such powerful educational, therapeutic, and decision-making modalities, process groups have the potential to do as much harm as good. Indeed, more than a few people have been emotional casualties in groups because the leader was untrained or unprepared to handle critical situations. Leading process groups thus requires more skills and a higher degree of leadership competence than merely moderating a faculty meeting or taking over the PTO board in the absence of the president. Peer pressure, forced conformity, less control, and increased complexity all contribute to a situation in which a principal can quickly feel over his or her head if not adequately prepared.

These disadvantages and advantages are summarized in Table 5.1.

TABLE 5.1 Advantages and Disadvantages of Group Work

Advantages	Disadvantages
Uses resources more efficiently	Confidentiality difficult to enforce
Encourages intimacy	Requires more skill and competence
Provides support system	Forces conformity and peer pressure
Teaches skills for interpersonal success	Individuals receive less help and attention
Provides opportunities for vicarious learning	Leader has less control and influence
Helps individuals practice new behaviors	Casualties can occur
Provides honest feedback	
Makes the principal's job more satisfying	

If you wish to lead process group activities in your school to facilitate the development of students as well as staff and parents, you should keep several things in mind:

1. Don't attempt any structure without assistance and/or supervision from someone who has expertise in the use of process groups (such as a school counselor, social worker, psychologist, colleague, or consultant).
2. Do not force participants to disclose personal material beyond what they feel is comfortable. Casualties are most likely to occur when people do more than they are ready to do.
3. Because peer pressure is so strong in groups, the individual rights of each participant need to be protected.
4. Understand clearly that there are specific times when you as a leader must intervene to protect the safety of group members and to ensure that your groups run smoothly.

When to Intervene in Groups

Research on effective group leadership has identified instances when you will need to do something specific to prevent people from getting hurt or to move the process along. We recommend that you memorize this list, or at least keep it close enough to refer to, until you log considerable experience as process leader. Intervention is called for under the following circumstances:

1. *To stop abusive behavior or hostility.* It is never permissible for group members to be disrespectful or abusive toward one another. Whenever you witness that one or more participants are treating others in ways that may be hurtful, you must step in to help redirect the tone: "Candy, how might you tell Frank the same thing but this time in a way that will not hurt his feelings? Then perhaps you, Frank, could tell Candy how you are feeling right now."

2. *To enforce rules that have been agreed on.* The usual way of beginning any process group is to create and negotiate rules of conduct regarding what behavior is acceptable and what is not. Generally, some guidelines are developed regarding confidentiality, speaking only for yourself, being respectful and caring during interactions, to name but a few. The leader's role is not so much to enforce these rules as to ensure that group members comply with them: "I notice that Danny has come in late again. How do you guys want to handle this?" Holding adults accountable and helping them to take leadership in holding group members accountable is challenging. These skills must be nurtured, practiced, and affirmed. Most adults will mumble and grumble to themselves or others rather than holding a peer accountable (either privately or publicly).

3. *To cut off distractions and digressions.* Because group time is so valuable and there is so much to do, the leader serves an important function by keeping things on track and not permitting any single member to dominate or control discussions. Some individuals also need direct feedback regarding their interpersonal styles that may be irritating or counterproductive: "Fred, I notice that you were rolling your eyes skyward as Jon was talking. Perhaps you could be helpful to him and let him know how you react when he takes so long to get his points across." Again, you must use great skill and tact when cutting off distractions and digressions with adults.

4. *To model appropriate ways of being.* One of the most powerful roles that you can play as a group leader is to demonstrate the particular ways in which you want children to act. This modeling can take place in the ways you present yourself, the skills you demonstrate, the confidence and serenity you exude, or even the language you use to express yourself: "Notice that I just said that I upset myself over what just happened, meaning that nobody else did this to me; I did it to myself based on the way I interpreted the situation. When I speak like that I am reminding myself that, ultimately, I am in control of how I choose to feel."

5. *To spice up boredom or passivity.* Groups, like classrooms and schools, can become predictable and stale without some intervention on the part of the leader to stir things up occasionally. There are no limits to the creative actions that you can take to breathe some life into a group—using humor, spontaneous actions, role-playing, almost anything to get children's energy flowing: "OK, you guys are acting like you are asleep. Let's try something a little different. I want each one of you to pretend to be someone else in this group for the next 15 minutes but don't say who you are imitating. Let's see if any of us can recognize ourselves."

Your faculty will respond to creativity and spontaneity as well. Take a few minutes at your next faculty meeting to create a "gallery of compliments." Create one "picture" for each staff member using a 10 × 18 sheet of construction paper. Pass the sheets around the room until everyone has had the opportunity to write a one sentence statement affirming something special about every person.

6. *To correct irrational or distorted thinking.* In one of the previous examples, we mentioned that the language people used is symptomatic of what they are thinking inside. By changing the ways we talk to ourselves, we also change our perceptions and subsequent actions based on these interpretations. It is thus common for group leaders to intervene when individuals speak in self-defeating or irrational ways:

Externalizing: "No matter what I do around here, somebody's always trying to get in my way."

Exaggerating: "This is the worst week I've ever had in teaching; actually, it's the worst week of my life."

Self-judging: "I'm a terrible teacher."

Denying responsibility: "It's not my fault. I just have bad luck."

Distorting: "If I don't get what I want, I'll quit."

In each case, the group leader jumps in to correct the way the child or adult is expressing himself or herself: "You mean that if you don't get what you want, you will be slightly disappointed."

7. *To reinforce disclosures.* Similar to classroom behavior modification, whenever a child or adult does something that we want to continue, and want others to imitate, we reinforce that behavior. "Tammy, I really like the way you just asserted yourself, and yet you did so in a very diplomatic and gentle way." We may also wish to systematically support behaviors such as disclosing, being direct and concise, cooperativeness, caring, and taking constructive risks.

8. *To provide structure as needed.* Groups flounder when they have either too much structure or not enough direction. Initially, when leaders make the transition from a formal classroom setting or a traditional meeting structure to process group settings, they tend to be too controlling in trying to ensure a successful experience. There are also times when groups meander because participants are not sure what is expected. Generally, it is better to provide more structure in the beginning stages of groups and then eventually allow individuals to assume more and more responsibility for where things go. Groups that have functioned together well for a period of time will have well-developed process skills.

9. *To stop complaining.* Once individuals feel safe, it does not take long for things to turn into a "gripe session." Kids will complain about other teachers, their parents, the weather, lost opportunities, and any number of possibilities, and this litany of injustices is often not helpful. Teachers will complain about kids, parents, budgets, and you (if you're out of earshot). Parents will complain about teachers, taxes, and their kids. One important rule is to talk only about things that we can do something about: "David, I appreciate the fact that it is hard for you with the reputation that you have created. We can't do anything about the past now, nor can we stop other people from saying what they don't like about you, but we sure can help you to act differently in the future. Let's concentrate on that instead." Focus on the "alterable variables," those situations and problems over which you have control.

10. *To comfort someone who is feeling anxious.* At times we sense the beginning signs that an individual is really struggling with something. Tears are on the verge of flowing. We observe agitation or withdrawal or anger seething. Intervention is sometimes required to make sure that such an individual feels supported: "Susan, you look like you are having a really hard time right now. How can we help you?" "Mark, I sense that this discussion is really difficult for you. Can we stop for a second and give you some more information to help you understand what we're talking about?"

11. *To confront inconsistencies.* Direct confrontation is in order whenever someone is doing something that is self-defeating or self-contradicting. Whereas we might model these interventions initially, after a while others pick up the tune, and then they can do the work themselves, especially with cues from the leader: "Cassandra, you look puzzled by what Nathan is saying, as if something doesn't fit right with what he said earlier. Why don't you tell him what you heard?" "I think we need to back-pedal to John's issue again. I have the feeling we moved on too quickly."

12. *To give constructive feedback.* Similar to modeling direct confrontation when indicated, we also want to demonstrate ways to give others the benefit of how we observe them. After we have given such feedback a few times, both children and adults pick up the behavior and continue doing it for one another. Ideally, feedback is most constructive when it is specific, phrased sensitively, and comes with a supporting example: "Dana, one reason why you aren't taken very seriously is the way you express yourself. You don't make eye contact, you giggle a lot, and put yourself down as you speak. Can anyone else offer Dana some ideas about how she sabotages herself?"

As you add group process interventions to your repertoire of skills make sure to reflect feelings and content as well as summarize what people say at various junctures.

Varieties of Group Process for Children

Teachers routinely incorporate group process activities into their curricula in a number of ways. They do so to spice up their classes, to supplement academic learning with emotional growth experiences, and to help children deal with the important issues they are struggling with such as peer acceptance, personal identity, values clarification, moral and emotional development, relationship problems, stress management, and other adjustment difficulties that are part of daily life.

As the principal, you can also play an active role in establishing and facilitating groups. For example, a child approaches you because she is upset about a friend whose mother was killed in a car accident, but you have noticed that several others seem to have been profoundly affected.

Some children seem more reticent than usual. Others have been acting out more than normal. Several parents have also reported that their children have expressed an unusual amount of worry about their safety. In such circumstances, talking about the accident openly, especially in relation to children's fears, is appropriate. This is just one example of how a process group experience might be used to help children clarify and express their feelings. Other examples of process groups follow.

As the leader of your school, you may find an issue or problem that is schoolwide: fighting on the playground, manners in the lunchroom, motivation to do homework, gang activity in the neighborhood, competition over conspicuous displays of material possessions, drug usage in the district, or lack of respect for teachers and other staff members. Groups can be formed that are specific to a single problem, to a class of children, or to a grade level. Process activities can be used to resolve conflict (e.g., a group of sixth graders who have brought their neighborhood rivalry to school), help children deal with a similar problem they have in common (a group of intermediate students with ability but no motivation), or to solve a schoolwide problem (e.g., stealing).

Structured Group Activities for Students

These kinds of exercises are quite familiar to you as ones your teachers use to help students personalize class material. The activities can be as simple as dividing a class into subgroups to discuss how they feel about a film they viewed, a book they read, or music they heard, or they can be as elaborate as a series of structured values clarification exercises that take place throughout a week, semester, or year. Usually, specific outcomes are desired, ones that help children achieve greater self-awareness and understanding of others.

Imagine, for example, that a social studies teacher is presenting a unit on discrimination. She might give her students a series of activities designed to help them become aware of their own prejudices and how such prejudices develop. An art teacher might show her students a painting and ask them to respond to it aesthetically.

The "tribes" model of cooperative learning is based on a set of structured group norms that emphasize sharing personal concerns and feelings, expressing positive regard for one another, and working as a team to complete assigned tasks. Rules are established for all interactions in which (a) confidentiality is enforced, (b) attentive listening to one another is required, (c) negative remarks are avoided, and (d) participants have the right to personal privacy. These group norms are intended to create a "tribal" community among students that makes it safe to explore new areas, express creativity, and develop intimacy without fear of criticism, rejection, or failure.

Consistent with process groups, responsibility is shifted from the teacher to the students to enforce the rules, draw one another out in discussion, and initiate interaction. The leader's role is to facilitate the process by providing structure, exploring issues, asking questions, introducing activities, and assigning tasks as indicated. The goals are to encourage responsible and caring behavior.

Fishbowl Structures

The principal works with a smaller group of children in the middle of the room with the rest of the class forming a circle around them. The observers may be assigned a "partner" inside the group to observe and give feedback to afterward, or they may be given certain observational tasks regarding the group process itself.

The participants inside the "fishbowl" are afforded a more intimate experience in which they demonstrate principles that the observers can also learn vicariously. After a round of this, observers and participants switch roles.

Two sections of sixth graders were assembled in the gymnasium to talk about their lack of respect for classified staff members (lunchroom supervisors, custodians, and secretaries). Students volunteered to play the roles of these individuals and other students acted out their roles. A spirited discussion then ensued with the entire group, with everyone reflecting on how terrible it felt to be treated rudely (or to watch someone else being treated badly—even if it was only just pretend). The students resolved to be more caring and sensitive to the people who come to school to serve them.

Guidance Groups

If school counselors had the time, the resources, and the support staff, they would devote most of their time to guidance groups and hence reap the most benefits for children. Kids need help with many areas that are not part of the academic curriculum: friendships (how to get them and keep them), how to get along with parents, and how to deal with stresses at home (divorce, separation, loss of jobs, drug and alcohol abuse), as well as coping with challenges at school (avoiding fights, study skills, peer acceptance).

Guidance groups are geared toward supplementing children's learning in academic subjects with specialized training in more pragmatic areas of immediate interest. This format is more familiar to you than many of the other kinds of groups because it offers primarily didactic instruction.

Whether designed to address problem solving or study skills, career exploration, or communication skills, this group format allows you to present practical information about a subject of great interest to children and then help them to individualize what they learned to their own unique situations.

Support Groups

A group of teachers in one school district became alarmed by the number of children who reported violence in their neighborhoods. They observed that many of the academic and discipline problems they encountered seemed to be triggered by what the children were experiencing in their communities. With the counselors in their district overworked and understaffed, the principal and teachers resolved to institute several measures to address the problem.

Support groups were organized under the guidance of the counselor. The teachers, as well as the principal, were prepared in teams of two coleaders and assigned to begin support groups in their schools. In addition to the problem of violence, another major problem was identified in the area of drug/alcohol abuse. Groups were thus targeted to these two different interest areas and followed a "curriculum" that consisted of providing opportunities for students to talk about their common concerns; to receive feedback from one another about what works and what doesn't; to learn they are not alone in their struggles, that others share their fears and apprehensions; and finally, to lend support to each other during these times of stress.

Structured Group Activities for Adults

Although many of the aforementioned group structures are designed for students, they may also be adapted for parents, teachers, or adult members of the community. In addition, several other process-oriented groups may be organized for staff members.

Conflict Resolution Activities

Conflicts are inevitable when a group of adults works closely with one another in the school setting. The stakes are high: student's lives. The problems are complex and not easily solved. Add to this mix the usual family and personal issues that each staff member will bring to the table.

Conflicts are even more likely when parents are added to the equation, either as members of a school leadership team or site-based council, or in a parent-teacher group like PTO.

Group conversation is a process that has been used in community groups to bring people together who traditionally have encountered barriers and roadblocks because of their differing ages, races, social status, ethnic backgrounds, religious backgrounds, economic levels, and educational levels. This process is especially appropriate when a group needs to take time away from the task and focus on developing interpersonal relationships and connections.

The "school" family at Meadow School was newly constituted. The beauty of their brand-new building did little to camouflage the distrust and hostility among several constituencies. The teachers were drawn from schools around the district, each with his or her own reasons for requesting a transfer. The principal was a new hire. One group of parents lived in expensive homes in a subdivision of rolling hills. A second group of parents might be considered disadvantaged and their children at risk, but they clearly wanted more for their children than they had been able to attain in school previously.

The group conversation process was perfect to bring this disparate group together. The principal consulted with a professional facilitator and together they structured the experiences. The facilitator was hired to do one pilot session and to observe the principal doing a second one independently. Thereafter, the principal was responsible for each group session.

Several sessions were held because the ideal size for a group conversation is no more than 40 participants. This structure is a way of matching experiences around a topic of common interest. It is totally different from the kind of group discussion we have when a problem is to be considered. Conversations will focus on topics such as Red-Letter Days, Family Holidays, Rebellion, Then and Now, or Favorite Family Foods. The choice of topic for discussion should be made in consultation with two or three key members of various subgroups in the larger school community. The leader functions as a "weaver" throughout the conversation as various group members share memories or experiences. A translator must be available if more than one language is spoken.

Consensus-Building Activities

The *parking lot meeting process* legitimatizes a practice that goes on anyhow: not saying what's really on your mind in a meeting or group (e.g., sitting silently, avoiding eye contact, appearing uptight) and then going out to the parking lot and saying what you really think. This is a good process to use when you feel a decision-making session is going poorly. If the participants are not speaking openly, if the climate is strained, and if people are weighing everything they say very carefully, this process will get the issues on the table. Some principals have even sent small groups of people out to the parking lot on a nice day to really talk about how they're feeling. Once everyone has had a chance to talk, convene all groups and ask each parking lot group to share the substance of its discussion with the entire group. Select a recorder to list all of the problems/concerns mentioned on chart paper. Deal with the issues that were raised in the parking lot meeting and proceed to making a decision or solving a problem.

Getting Support for Yourself

The best way to learn to lead process groups is to recruit a colleague who knows more than you do. With a more experienced coleader, you will appease many of your justifiable apprehensions about venturing into this unknown territory and also provide yourself a safety net when the going gets tough. A coleader can model for you alternative ways to begin, maintain, and end group experiences. He or she can also give you valuable feedback after each session regarding aspects of your leadership style that you can work to improve.

Whether you find this partner among your own colleagues—a counselor, administrator, school psychologist, or teacher—or whether you invite someone from the local university to supervise you in the field, a coleader will give you the added boost of confidence and support necessary when undertaking an exciting yet challenging new adventure.

Suggested Activities

1. Observe the dynamics and processes that take place in the groups to which you currently belong—at school, in your administrative team, at home, and in your community, church, or synagogue. What characteristic roles do you play in these groups? What are your strengths and weaknesses as a group member and potential leader? Note these reactions in a journal or share them aloud in a group discussion.

2. Select a structured group activity that accesses children's values, feelings, and beliefs—especially one that you would feel comfortable implementing. Try out this activity with a group of children, classmates, or friends. Solicit feedback from them afterward as to what they liked and disliked about the experience.

3. Identify someone who has experience leading groups and who may agree to work with you as a coleader of a support group. Approach the person (a school counselor, school psychologist, school social worker, senior colleague with advanced training, a counselor educator from the local university) with a plan for the kind of group you might like to run.

4. Meet in a group with your peers and share experiences you have had as members of process groups. What did you learn from these experiences? What specific things did the leader(s) do that you most and least appreciated?

Suggested Readings

Corey, G., & Corey, M. S. (1997). *Groups: Process and practice* (5th ed.). Pacific Grove, CA: Brooks/Cole.

Forester-Miller, H., & Kottler, J. A. (1997). *Issues and challenges for group practitioners.* Denver, CO: Love.

Gibbs, J. (1987). *Tribes: A process for social development and cooperative learning.* Santa Rosa, CA: Center Source.

McEwan, E. K. (1997). *Leading your team to excellence: How to make quality decisions.* Thousand Oaks, CA: Corwin.

Rohnke, K. (1984). *Silverbullets: A guide to initiating problems, adventure games and trust activities.* Dubuque, IA: Kendall/Hunt.

6

Being Skillful in
Parent Conferences

Conferences with parents are an almost daily part of the life of an elementary school principal. These encounters are very different from those conducted by teachers on a regular basis to talk about a student's progress or problems in school. Although there are certainly exceptions, most parents visit the principal when they have a problem.

Mrs. Jeffreys isn't happy with Tammy's teacher. Mrs. Turner's homework assignments are too confusing and she expects too much of students when they also have outside activities. Mrs. Jeffreys has tried to talk to the teacher but feels dissatisfied with what she was able to accomplish. Tammy continues to struggle with homework. Mrs. Jeffreys wants you to talk to the teacher and tell her to change.

The Stevens family is worried about the reading list for the upcoming Battle of the Books, a program cosponsored by the public library. They feel there are too many books on the list that have questionable themes and plots. They want you to get the list revised.

Mr. Marklund is sure there must be an organized plot against his son, Tom. He's being picked on at the bus stop, in the lunchroom, and on the playground. He wants you to do something to make other children nicer to him. He wants you to provide better supervision so that Tom will feel safe. Otherwise he's going to stop sending Tom to school.

Of course, you may not be able to solve parents' problems for them, but you will be able to help them work through issues and come to conclusions about changes they can make in their own behavior. You won't be able to change the curriculum or fire the teacher that has them hopping mad, but you will be able to explore some options or facilitate a meeting between the parent and the teacher. You can't change their child into a popular, straight-A student overnight, but you can offer extra help, encouragement, and support at school to meet a child's social needs.

Developing the counseling and consulting skills that enable you to handle any parent conference with confidence and equanimity will increase your job satisfaction tremendously, reduce the stress you may have felt when confronted by difficult parents in the past, and build parental support for your school.

The Functions of Parent-Principal Conferences

Frequently, the thought of a parent conference puts an educator on the defensive. Questions like "What does this parent want from me?" and "Who does this parent think he is?" come to mind. And we ready a list of retorts such as "I trust all my teachers to have good judgment." "You're the only parent to complain about that assignment, Mrs. Jones." "We have plenty of supervision on our playground." Yet, more often than not, conferences are helpful and motivating.

Parents want their children to do well. They want educators to help their children. The information they give, whether willingly offered or skillfully obtained in an interview, provides you with important insights that allow you to plan accordingly.

Directing a Constructive Conference

In many ways, a parent conference is like an improvisational play: There is a general script to follow but with lots of room for spontaneous action. You are the director as well as one of the main characters. The parents and/or the child form the rest of the cast, although they may be unclear about their roles. Each of you is probably rehearsing a part in anticipation of what the other might say or do. Careful thought will need to be given to every facet of the production for the performance to go smoothly.

Setting the stage. Just as there are different kinds of plays—dramas, musicals, comedies—so is there an assortment of principal-parent conferences, each with its own unique plot development and script structure. Essentially, conferences come about in three ways: (a) initiated by the parent (if there is a perceived problem), (b) initiated by school personnel (if a consultation may help to gather information or solicit assistance), and (c) initiated by the system (regularly scheduled meetings each semester). Depending on who initiates the meeting, your objectives will be somewhat different. But whatever the goals of the meeting or the problems that are brought to the table, there are important attitudes and behaviors that you as a principal can exhibit that will ensure more productive meetings with parents. Effective instructional leaders have learned that what they *are* speaks far more eloquently than what they *say* and so, in addition to acquiring the skills that enable them to work well with parents, they attend to personal issues of character.

Ways to Be

Be trustworthy. You can't make people trust you. They either do or they don't based on your behavior, your reputation, or experiences they've had with someone in the same position as yours. Some parents may reserve judgment until they've seen you in action themselves, others will take the word of a friend or neighbor (the grapevine is alive and well), and still others will make up their minds about you immediately based on nothing more than a "gut feeling." Building trust among parents (as well as staff members and students) is one of the most important tasks you will undertake as an administrator. Trust is the glue that holds any relationship together through tough times. When parents trust you, they will give you the benefit of the doubt. They will approach you with an attitude of respect that says, "Even though I'm upset with you personally or have questions about the way things are done here, I know that you're an intelligent, caring person who will try to understand where I'm coming from."

Have integrity. Having integrity, the second important trait of character that gives you "money in the problem-solving bank," consists of far more than just telling the truth. Integrity speaks of a unity and consistency of personal behavior that withstands the scrutiny and invites the confidence of parents. Educators of integrity are predictable because they make decisions out of a seamless and coherent set of values and beliefs. They know what they stand for and can articulate their beliefs with eloquence.

Things to Do

In addition to having trustworthiness and integrity, there are many things you can do in your interactions with parents that can defuse distress, tension, and anger. Shake hands and welcome parents into your office. Even the most hostile parents will warm up to a personal greeting, an engaging smile, and a welcoming touch.

Sit eye to eye and knee to knee. This simple statement is a key principle of group dynamics. It means that people need proximity to one another to engage in problem solving. When people are seated too far away from one another, the space between them inhibits communication. Don't sit behind your desk when meeting with parents. Sit side by side at a round table that could include other participants if needed. Provide comfortable chairs and offer coffee, water, or a soft drink (if available) to put parents at ease. Close the door so people can speak freely and make sure all phone calls and interruptions are held. These simple behaviors will send the message before a word is spoken that you value and respect parents.

Listen. The very first thing to do when a parent with a problem comes to call is to listen. Of course, you know that listening is a whole lot more than just hearing the words that someone is speaking. Their facial expressions, bodily movements, and tone of voice can communicate volumes about their true feelings.

- Notice the attitudes and feelings that are expressed. They may communicate something different from what the words are saying. Posture, eye movements, hand gestures, tone of voice, and facial expressions are powerful communicators.
- Listen "between the lines" for what a parent is not saying in addition to what is being said. Decode the underlying message that is being communicated. For example, when a parent says, "It's not that I have a problem with the way this was

handled," what she's really saying is: "I have a definite problem with the way this was handled."

- Do not respond with your own message by evaluating, sympathizing, giving your opinion, offering advice, analyzing, or questioning. Simply report back what you heard in the message as well as the attitudes and the feelings that were expressed.

- Keep your body language in harmony with openness, receptiveness, and attentiveness. Maintain eye contact, sit quietly without fidgeting, and arrange your hands and arms in a nonthreatening way. Don't frown, look alarmed, or make faces. Nod your head occasionally to indicate you understand the speaker.

- Make occasional and appropriate verbal responses like "Oh," "Hmm," or "Uh-huh" to confirm to the speaker that you are paying attention. Parents need to feel that you are understanding them both emotionally (e.g., their feelings of anger or fear) and intellectually (the actual words they are saying).

- Keep listening until there is a sign that the speaker has finished speaking and is ready to listen to you.

- Take notes about what the individual is telling you. Explain to the person that you are taking notes to help you remember critical details of the conversation. Most people with problems will be relieved to know that someone is finally listening to them and cares enough to write it down.

Open your mind. Parents who are troubled and frightened often need permission and acceptance to share their private and very deeply felt concerns. If they sense that an educator isn't interested, doesn't care, or is passing premature judgment, they may well get cold feet and leave your office without having articulated the real problem. Parents need the freedom to explore an issue without criticism or censure. In the process, you may be exposed to a new point of view or an alternative way of viewing education, so suspend your initial prejudice or distaste and become a learner.

Keep calm; remain confident. To change a difficult person, you must first change yourself—your way of thinking about the person and your way of responding to the familiar provocations. Most of us find it difficult to be neutral about parents who are angry and hostile.

They bring out the worst in us. Maintaining your composure will effectively dismantle the hostile feedback loop that can be created if you respond in kind to angry words. If you're pleasant and friendly, you will, in the long run, wear them down, even get them to be cordial back. Your composure and courtesy will act as a mirror in which parents will find their own desperate attempts to intimidate and abuse embarrassingly and unattractively reflected. When parents sense your confidence, and they will, their bluster and bravado will diminish. If they sense fear and uncertainty, they will go for your jugular.

Set boundaries. Establish a specific ending time for a meeting prior to its beginning and you will find it easier to keep the discussion focused. If parents think they have an unlimited amount of time to state their case, they will take every bit of it.

There is a difference between being tolerant and accepting and enabling abusive behavior. No matter how upset parents might be, they have no right to speak to you disrespectfully. Rather than arguing or yelling back at a parent who is out of control, explain that it isn't acceptable to speak to you in that manner.

Apologize. Sometimes the first words from your mouth when a parent stops talking long enough to "come up for air" should be an apology. In these litigious days, many educators are loathe to utter those words, fearing lawsuits and damages, but not saying you're sorry when you are obviously at fault will only exacerbate an already difficult situation.

Accept blame. Often if you're willing to take your share, parents will back down and admit they or their child might also be at fault.

Get to the point. See if you can get past the anger and frustration a parent brings to your office to the real issues and the bottom line request. Often this can be accomplished with a simple question when all of the grievances and concerns have been aired: "What do you want to see happen as a result of this conference?" If a parent cannot answer that question directly, then more discussion is needed.

Empathize. Learn to lay aside your own needs to be heard and understood and focus instead on hearing and understanding what parents have to say. Perhaps you have never had the identical experience they are having, but suspend belief for a moment and imagine yourself in their shoes. How would you feel? How would you act? Where would you go for help? Suppose your child were being evaluated for mental retardation. Would you be calm, trusting, and totally relaxed? Suppose your child were being bullied on the playground and you thought no one cared. Would you take it lying down? Probably not. If you sincerely engage in this exercise of imagination, the parents with whom you are meeting will feel your empathy and begin to relax.

Ask questions. Learn the power of asking the right questions to uncover all aspects of a problem. This process can be compared to the party gag of putting a small gift-wrapped box in increasingly larger and larger boxes, wrapping each one more elaborately than the last. Just when the person who is doing the unwrapping thinks he's about to get his "real" present, he discovers that the final box is empty. Sometimes in talking with parents something similar will happen. Once all of the layers of confusion and misinformation have been peeled away, the problem may be nonexistent. Ask all the usual "who, what, where, and why" questions. You may also find it helpful to use statements like "I'm not sure I understand. Help me to see why this is so important to you." When all else fails, ask for the parents' advice: "If you were in my place, what would you do?" Don't be afraid of asking open-ended questions to which you have no suitable answers. But beware of assuming the role of prosecuting attorney in your questioning mode. Clarification, not conviction, is your ultimate goal.

Sometimes strange and surprising things can happen if you are able to lay aside your own mental models (or paradigms) and consider alternatives. The notion that a conference with a distressed parent might actually turn out to be a learning experience for you as the administrator may be a somewhat revolutionary idea to consider, but drop your defenses and give it a try.

Speak gently. The tone and quality of your voice are just as important as the words you speak. If you are hurried, hostile, defensive, or distracted, your voice will give you away immediately and parents will judge you to be insincere, even if you're saying all the right things. There is an Old Testament proverb that says, "A soft answer turns away wrath, but a harsh word stirs up anger." A soft answer means that you don't contradict, correct, condescend, or disagree with parents who are already infuriated, even if they are obviously totally misinformed. Here are some other things to do when speaking to parents.

- Meet parents on a personal level. Say something positive about their child. If possible, do your homework before the meeting. Look at the student's cumulative folder and consult with specialists (art, music, physical education, computer, learning center) to determine any special gifts or talents. One genuine compliment will help to set a positive tone for the conference.

- At the close of the conference, summarize what you think you've heard. Not only is this a good faith gesture that lets parents know you fully understand their point of view, but a brief review of critical information will clear up any misconceptions that may exist on either side of the table.

- Conclude all conferences with a clear understanding of what was agreed on and what if any action you and/or the parents will take. Ask parents if they are satisfied that their problem has been heard and understood. Even if the conference concludes without consensus, the knowledge that they have been heard and understood will defuse even the most anxious parents. Be sure to keep careful notes of the action items for immediate follow-up.

Redirect. Parents who are perturbed often want the principal or other administrator to do their "homework" for them. Suppose Mr. and Mrs. X are upset with Teacher Q. Rather than calling the teacher themselves to discuss the issue, they approach you and demand that the problem be solved for them. Your first question should always be: "Have you talked to the teacher about this?" If the answer is "No, we don't want the teacher to know we're complaining," then it's time to let the parents know that you'll be sharing exactly what they've said with the teacher anyway and it would be far better for them to do it. If the answer to the question is yes, and the parents can document several attempts on their part to solve the problem with no success, then it's appropriate for you to step in and facilitate between the teacher and parent and/or determine what is standing in the way of the problem being solved. But beware of being "triangulated" (i.e., caught in the middle of two people who should be talking to each other but instead have decided to put you in charge of their problems).

Lower the boom lightly. There is an art to giving bad news, something you may well be called on to do in the course of meeting with parents who are upset. How do you tell parents their child has no friends? How do you share the possibility that a child has a severe learning problem? How do you inform parents that their child is a thief and a liar? How do you communicate to parents who want to blame everything on you that they own a good share of the problem? Very carefully. With tact and gentleness. But with directness. Don't be so afraid of telling the truth that you never get to the point. Gauge how much information a parent can comprehend at one time, particularly if the information is coming as a complete surprise to them. Don't babble and generalize. Speak simply and give concrete examples.

Welcome constructive criticism. Perhaps the idea of welcoming constructive criticism from parents is as attractive to you as the prospect of oral surgery. But sometimes we need to hear and heed what parents have to say that might help us improve how we deliver education to their children. And, even when the criticism is more destructive than constructive, we need to listen and respond with openness, interest, and appreciation. If you've made a mistake, admit to it. State briefly what you (and/or your staff) have learned from the experience. Tell parents what you will do differently in the future to prevent the situation from happening again. Parents will respect you for your honesty and directness.

Don't react. Reacting is acting without thinking. There are many possible ways to react that are inappropriate. Sometimes our first inclination when cornered by an angry parent is to "strike back" (e.g., counterattack, defend, explain, justify, or just plain cut off and "divorce" parents we don't like). Instead, step back and remain neutral. Don't personalize the attack and try to convince the parent of their wrongness and your rightness. Equally ineffective is "giving in" just to get a parent out of your office and your hair, without regard for the child, any teachers who may be involved, or policies already in place to handle such situations. Be firm and stand your ground while solving problems. Having a reputation as a "wimpy" pushover is almost as bad as being labeled a "terrible tyrant."

Consider cultural differences in communication. When the parents with whom you are meeting come from a different cultural background than you do, try to understand the subtleties that dictate their nonverbal behaviors and communication patterns. Nonverbal signals to consider include distance between people, eye contact, and whether touching is expected or appropriate. Who should initiate the conversation, whether interrupting is acceptable, and how to bring up difficult topics are also important considerations. If you are aware of cultural differences, you can alter your behavior patterns to put parents at ease and increase the likelihood of productive problem solving.

Take your time. There is no rule that says every problem needs an immediate solution. Always take time to think; any decision (and/or upset parent) will benefit from a 24-hour cooling-off period. Never permit parents to back you into the "I've got to know what you're going to do now" corner. The wise administrator knows how to buy time and gather information. Here are some ways to "slow down the game":

- During the meeting, pause and say nothing to give yourself time to gather your thoughts. During a long pause you can sip your coffee or check your notes.
- Regroup by taking a few minutes to summarize the information or progress made thus far.
- Never commit to action that involves other individuals (especially teachers) without first consulting with them.
- Ask for time to gather more information or consult with a superior. This sends the message that you are serious about solving the problem but want to make sure you're fully informed.
- If you feel your temper flaring and your blood pressure soaring, tell parents that you need to check on something with your secretary. Step out of your office, take several deep breaths, smile, count to 10, and return to your office with your

composure restored. This is the administrative version of taking a time-out.

- When a meeting is headed nowhere (e.g., information is being
  repeated, tempers are beginning to flare, and nothing is being
  accomplished), perhaps it's time to schedule a follow-up session. Consider including some experts (e.g., a behavior management specialist to discuss some ways to improve time-on-
  task in the classroom or the librarian to explain the book
  selection policy of the district) to help the situation.

Don't fight 'em; join 'em. When parents identify a problem in your
school, enlist their help in solving it. A group of parents came to see
a principal about problems in his school's lunchroom. Instead of becoming defensive, he applauded the parents' interest, said he had
already been discussing what could be done to make it a more appe-
tizing experience for his students, and asked their help in creating a
task force to study the problem. Everyone came out winners in that
situation.

Give options to parents. Don't back them into corners. Help them
preserve their dignity. Allow them to save face. It's not about win-
ning or losing; it's about solving problems for the benefit of children
and their learning. Remember the goal.

Problems, not personalities. Stay focused on issues and keep people and their flaws and faults out of the discussion as much as possible. When parents start tearing down people, redirect their attention to solving the problem. Using these simple strategies, you'll be
able to handle most any parent who comes your way. And you'll do
it with wisdom, understanding, and patience.

When the Play Doesn't Go as Planned

Even the most experienced principals have difficulties at times.
Parents are not always as cooperative and pleasant as we would like
them to be. Single parents and working parents, for example, find it
difficult to schedule appointments. If a parent brings his or her own
personal problems to the conference, they might take priority over

the problems of the child. The parent may need a sounding board before he or she can look at the problems of the child. Sometimes interactions become heated and tempers flare. There may also be some resentment toward you as an authority figure or a representative of an institution viewed as repressive or uncaring. For these and other reasons, you will encounter parents who appear less interested in helping their child than they do in knocking you for a loop.

You may find yourself dealing with difficult parents who are either frightened and defensive or extremely aggressive and demanding. We will review examples and discuss strategies for working with such challenging parents.

The Angry Parent

"My daughter does not cheat, and I resent your accusing her!" Larisa had turned in a test paper with all of her answers identical to the student who sat next to her, a student who always got straight As. You must recognize that anger is often due to frustration. The best approach in this situation is to let the parent vent his or her feelings while you maintain an accepting attitude. This will be very hard to do because you will also be feeling angry for having your integrity questioned. Self-control, however, will serve you well. Use your reflection and listening skills until the anger loses its momentum. Don't argue or you will only aggravate matters further.

Change the focus of the discussion to one of problem solving in which you attempt to enlist the parent's help in resolving the difficulties. A general rule to keep in mind during any interpersonal struggle is this: When you are doing something that doesn't work, don't do it anymore; try something else. If trying to change the parent's mind isn't successful, rather than redoubling your efforts, try backing off instead. Try anything other than what isn't working. But do not, under any circumstances, let things escalate into a shouting match. Inner tranquility can best be maintained if you talk to yourself throughout the encounter, reminding yourself that this isn't personal, that the parent is just doing the best he or she can, and that nothing will be gained by trying to humiliate him or her.

Naturally, you must draw the line if the parent becomes disrespectful or abusive. At that point, suggest that a colleague join you as mediator. Rescheduling an appointment at another time is also effective because the parent will have had time to regain composure. We give you fair warning that no matter how conciliatory, easygoing, and nonconfrontational you may be, there will definitely come a time when a parent will jump all over you for no legitimate reason that you can identify. Try to prepare yourself for such an encounter in advance so that you are not so surprised that you cannot gather your wits about you and act professionally.

The Disappointed Parent

"I don't know what I can do," said Mrs. Cohen. She was disappointed that her son had received a D on his report card. "He's such a good boy. We had such high hopes for him, but he just doesn't seem to care about school." Parents can sabotage their children just as much by being overinvolved as by being neglectful. Some children feel a tremendous sense of power in being able to say to their parents, "You can't make me do anything that I don't want to do. And just to prove it, I will do the opposite of what you want."

Some parents also have unrealistic expectations for their children. Regardless of the child's interests or talents, the parents press him or her to live out their own aspirations. This is also likely to result in disappointment. Disappointed parents need someone who will hear them out. You can be of invaluable assistance by helping them to do a "reality check," comparing what they expect to what is possible. You can also help them to understand the degree to which they are imposing their own goals on their children, who may have agendas of their own. Finally, you can help them to sort out what they may be doing to contribute to the disappointing results. Helping parents to realize that nagging a child to do homework not only decreases the likelihood that it will be completed but actually guarantees that the child would rebel. Developing a contract that solicits the student's input and builds in personal accountability has a greater chance of success than nagging.

The Troubled Parent

"Jenny is just getting to be too much for me to handle. With all the things that have happened to me lately I just can't seem to concentrate very well. I know Jenny needs my help, but sometimes I just can't find the energy." The troubled parent needs someone outside his or her circle of family and friends to listen. In some situations, you will be viewed as a professional who is both compassionate and highly skilled—and you can do a lot for someone who is troubled by helping him or her feel understood. In most circumstances, however, your main task is to develop a trusting enough relationship with troubled parents so that they will respect your advice to get help from a professional. Depressed, anxious, or otherwise suffering parents are in no position to help their children. Your job is to urge them to consult a professional therapist or physician, if not for their own good then certainly for the benefit of children who are being short-changed.

The task of encouraging someone to seek professional help is not as easy as it sounds: People who are experiencing emotional difficulties are often resistant to the idea of seeing a mental health professional because of fears that they will be labeled "crazy." You can pave the way for parents by addressing their concerns and then firmly encouraging them to follow through with their resolve.

The Manipulative Parent

"I know you said on the phone that you couldn't change my daughter's report card, and I certainly respect your professional judgment in these matters, but. . . . " Not all parents you meet will be straightforward as to what they want from you; some will have hidden agendas that involve getting you to do things that you don't want to do or feel uncomfortable doing. The issue of changing grades is just one such example. Others may include the parent who wants you to give special preference to his or her child. Another may want you to make unreasonable arrangements or to accommodate inappropriate requests.

The intrinsic conflict of these situations is that some parents want something from you. They know that if the request is put to you directly, you will say no. So they resort to manipulative, devious, underhanded ways to get their way. Some of these parents will attempt to intimidate you by exploiting their power ("I have a good friend on the school board") or by threatening you ("I just may have to initiate disciplinary action against you if you persist in being so closed-minded about this").

There are no easy answers for dealing with manipulative parents. We mention this circumstance more as a reminder to you than as a situation that has definite solutions. We simply urge you to stand by your professional standards and not give in to manipulative ploys. But you must recognize what is happening before it is too late. Such awareness comes from experience.

Good supervision and support also are crucial, especially to you in the early part of your career—not only in learning the ins and outs of conducting parent conferences but in all facets of your work. When you encounter manipulative parents, you will need someone in your corner—a senior colleague, your superintendent, and some trusted teachers—someone who can lend support and advise you how to make it through the traps that have been set.

The Quiet Parent

This individual can be one of the most challenging parents with whom to connect in a conference. Because of nervousness, uncertainty about what is expected, or just a passive personality, some parents will sit throughout the conference and barely say a word. You may find yourself babbling to fill the time and then feel very uncomfortable about what took place. What to do with a quiet parent depends very much on why the person is reticent. Your first assignment, therefore, should be to try to make such a determination: "I notice that you are not saying very much." The parent will then clarify that he feels a little uncomfortable, or that he doesn't know what you expect, or that he just doesn't talk much. (You can verify the last assumption if he replies to your statement by saying, "Yup.")

In most cases, be patient so that the parent will come to know and trust you enough to open up a bit. Remember, however, that if you attempt to fill the silences with a nonstop monologue, then the parent will never have the chance to engage with you. Every conference has its own pace and distinct characteristics. If you remain sensitive and responsive to each parent's personality, then you can adapt your style of interaction to fit the unique requirements of the situation. In some conferences, the parent will do most of the talking; in others, you will take more of a direct lead. The more flexible you can be in the way you conduct conferences, the more likely that you will develop positive working relationships with a variety of parents from diverse cultures, backgrounds, and personal situations.

We do not wish to make you unduly apprehensive or mistrustful about the parents you will encounter. The vast majority will be cooperative, respectful, and very grateful for your high degree of dedication and competence. Be warned, however, that at least once a week you will probably meet at least one parent who will not be very pleasant for you to work with.

Multicultural Perspectives

Flexibility is indeed the key to building trust and respect in your relationships with parents. It requires knowledge of the diverse cultural backgrounds from which your children originate and a willingness on your part to do what it takes to help individuals with different values, needs, and interests feel comfortable. You have already learned the importance of multicultural sensitivity with respect to reaching children; the same principles apply to working with their parents.

You will need to learn about the attitudes and customs of the cultures from which your students come to (a) understand the behavior patterns of the children and their parents and (b) avoid problems of miscommunication. In particular, pay attention to nonverbal communication. For example, in many ethnic groups it is considered rude to look an adult in the eye. For this reason, people look down rather than at a speaker. Different attitudes toward competition explain why some students will turn to others for help during a test. Cooperation rather than competition may be emphasized at home. Certain cultures frown on women in authoritative roles. Consequently, a female principal may have difficulty establishing rapport with male parents without knowing why. Developing an appreciation and awareness of the various groups from which your students come will facilitate your interactions with them.

Suggested Activities

1. Explore the dynamics of your family history, noting the impact of your parents' conduct on your own behavior at school. Try to recall a specific instance in which something your parents did or said had a dramatic impact on your life. What could a principal have done to intervene with your parents on your behalf?

2. Recruit a few friends or colleagues to help you role-play a parent conference. Concentrate on applying the helping skills (especially questioning and active listening) during your interaction.

3. With your partners, you take on the role of an angry or defensive parent who feels threatened by the teacher's influence and authority over his or her child. After the interaction, talk about your feelings and reactions from the parent's point of view. What did it feel like to have your competence as a parent challenged?

4. Write a sample letter to parents describing the objectives of a conference. Include what you hope to accomplish, what the parents might expect to occur, where and when the meeting will take place, and what can be done in preparation.

5. Interview a sample of parents who have children of different ages. Ask them what their best and worst experiences have been in conferences with principals. Solicit their advice about some things that you might do differently.

6. Interview several experienced principals to ask about their favorite methods of leading parent conferences. Ask how they prepare for the meetings, how they keep themselves in control when they are being challenged, how they keep parents focused on the goals of the meeting, and how they use the time most effectively.

Suggested Readings

Kottler, J. A. (1992). *Compassionate therapy: Working with difficult clients*. San Francisco: Jossey-Bass.

Kottler, J. A. (1997). *Succeeding with difficult students*. Thousand Oaks, CA: Corwin.

Lawrence, G., & Hunter, M. (1995). *Parent-teacher conferencing*. Thousand Oaks, CA: Corwin.

McEwan, E. K. (1998). *How to deal with parents who are angry, troubled, afraid, or just plain crazy*. Thousand Oaks, CA: Corwin.

7

Consulting Effectively
With Other Professionals

No matter how knowledgeable and skilled you are in the counseling process; no matter how comfortable and adept you become in the various roles you play; and no matter how proficiently you are able to communicate with others, assess children's problems, understand their underlying issues, and design effective helping strategies, you will still need the assistance of a number of other professionals and specialists in your work. The best principals functioning in counseling roles are, in fact, those who can diagnose accurately that a problem exists and know where and to whom to turn for expert guidance. Consulting with others will enable you to

- Gain the benefit of expertise that is outside your specialty
- Look at fresh or innovative solutions to problems that you face
- Get a more detached and objective perspective on what you are experiencing
- Get help handling tasks that you do not have the time or inclination to complete
- Provide you with additional training in a particular area of need

Consulting With Teachers

Although you might like to ride in on your white steed to heroically rescue members of your school family who are in distress, don't overlook the talent and expertise in your teaching staff that is available to help you. Experienced and perceptive teachers can give you background information on a child or family of which you may be unaware, let you know about all the interventions they have tried that may come as a surprise to you, and share their professional insights. Become receptive to consulting with your staff and you will empower both your teachers and yourself.

Consulting With Colleagues

Being a principal is sometimes such a lonely job. So much of the time, you are the one who makes the decisions and then lives with the consequences. Even though you may have a wide network of friends and acquaintances within the school, there are still limits to what you can reveal. You must always be concerned about showing favoritism, and so many of the things you reflect on and struggle with you keep to yourself. You are thus prevented from learning as much as you could from your actions because it is so rare you get feedback from peers.

Identify a mentor among your administrative colleagues, an individual whose counseling and consulting skills you admire and whose personality and temperament are suited to helping you. This individual could be your superintendent or supervisor, a fellow principal, a faculty member at the local university, or someone in a staff position in central office.

Relationships such as this are not built overnight; trust builds slowly. Of course, you can help the process along and not just wait for the other person to make the overtures. Invite them to lunch and ask for their advice when dealing with a particularly difficult situation. Gauge their willingness to take the time and energy needed to be a mentor. Although some individuals may have a great deal of personal expertise, they may not have the time or the willingness to share it with others.

Mary Stevens is a brand-new principal and is looking for someone who can help her do a more effective job with parental problem solving. She has observed the director of special education, Barbara Arest, at several meetings and has been impressed with the way she has been able to defuse potentially explosive situations. She seems to have just the right words to make teachers feel appreciated and willing to work harder. Mary decides to take the director to lunch and ask for her input.

Consulting With Counselors

It was hard for John Blane to describe the changes he had noticed in Dylan. He was maybe a little quieter, a bit more pensive than usual at the weekly lunches they enjoyed together at McDonald's, a reward for completed homework. The principal and fifth grader had been working on a contract since the beginning of the school year and Mr. Blane was excited about the changes he'd seen in Dylan's sense of responsibility. But something was different about Dylan's energy level today. Mr. Blane couldn't quite put his finger on it. His attempts to communicate with Dylan were quickly cut off. "How's it going?" was answered with the typical, "Fine." "How are you today?" "Good." End of conversation. He decided to talk to the counselor who saw Dylan weekly and ask her if she would discreetly talk to him.

A few days later, the counselor reported that there were indeed some problems in the family, things that Dylan preferred remained confidential. The counselor expressed gratitude for Mr. Blane's perceptive observations and reassured him that everything was once again under control. Mr. Blane was still intensely curious about what had happened with Dylan and his family, but the counselor explained that sometimes children have a difficult time sharing troubles with someone they admire. In this case, because Dylan liked Mr. Blane so much, he didn't want him to know anything about him that did not show him in the best light. Sometimes it happens that although we want to be helpful to students, our authority role prevents us from developing the kind of relationship that counselors are perfectly positioned and trained to create.

Sometimes you may consult with a counselor informally, such as in the case of Mr. Blane. Other times it may be best to handle the situation yourself with the guidance of the counselor. In either instance, counselors can be among your best resources in addressing the emotional needs of your students, and of yourself.

Because a little learning can be a dangerous thing, you would also not wish to usurp the responsibilities and expertise of the counselor assigned to your school. You might be perceived (and function) as a meddler, an amateur, as someone who can do more harm than good when you attempt to handle cases that are beyond your level of counseling skills. On the other hand, counselors will be very grateful for any principal who truly understands the value of what they do.

Seeing a Counselor as
Your Personal Consultant

A unique feature of counseling as a profession is that a person does not need to have an emotional disorder or even a "problem" to seek help. Whereas other mental health professionals such as psychiatrists, psychologists, and social workers specialize in treating severe mental disorders, counselors are experts in helping people with normal concerns of daily living. This includes, but is not limited to, adjustment problems or transitions to life changes, career development, finding meaning in one's life, developing better self-understanding, resolving relationship difficulties, planning for the future, reducing stress, and any other struggle that human beings face as a part of daily existence.

Although education is a very rewarding profession, it is also a stressful one—filled with demands, responsibilities, and commitments that sometimes seem beyond what any person could reasonably be expected to handle. As an authority figure, you will be a target for some children who wish to act out their frustration and hostility. Sometimes you will be caught in a tug-of-war between teachers, parents, and children, with no apparent escape in sight. Furthermore, the burnout rate in administration is high because of what is expected from you.

Deciding to seek the services of a counselor as your personal consultant can therefore help you in a number of ways:

1. An experience as a client can help you improve your own helping skills. By watching a professional at work, by noting what works best with you, you will find yourself unconsciously and deliberately adopting strategies to your own situations.

2. You will have a safe, confidential support system that will give you the opportunity to work through stresses and concerns without having to burden your family and friends.

3. You can motivate yourself to grow and to continue learning about those aspects of your functioning you wish to improve.

4. You can work through particular difficulties that crop up in your life. Issues that educators are especially vulnerable to include a fear of failure, feelings of uncertainty as to whether

the rewards of the profession are worth the aggravation, feelings of stagnation, and conflicts with colleagues or teachers.

5. You can counteract the deleterious effects of school life. On a regular basis you will be dealing with children who do not necessarily want to be within your control or domain; some will fight you every inch of the way. The wear and tear takes its toll until, eventually, you will start to feel serious effects— unless, of course, you have developed coping skills to help you stay energized.

Many of these reasons for consulting a counselor are evident in the testimony of one beginning administrator who was an outstanding classroom teacher, yet encountered a number of adjustment difficulties during her first year on the job:

I really had no idea how hard it would be for me to finish my first year as a principal. Several times I wanted to quit. In fact, I probably would have quit if I hadn't seen a counselor during some difficult times. My superintendent had very high expectations for student achievement and I really felt a lot of pressure to turn the school around.

The parents were up-in-arms about a change in parking regulations; the teachers were resentful that the superintendent didn't choose the candidate they wanted to get hired for the job, and my kids chose the exact same time to quit doing chores and their homework.

I was always so organized as a teacher. My lesson plans were models for my team. Nothing prepared me for the chaos I had to deal with—teachers who were totally ineffective, kids who weren't reading on grade level, and parents who cared even less. I was totally demoralized and started to consider other career options.

At the suggestion of a friend, I started seeing a counselor recommended to me by a colleague I trusted. At first, I didn't much like it at all. I kept it a secret because I thought people might think I was going crazy—actually, that is how it felt to me.

But then it started to feel so good to have somebody I could talk to, someone who didn't judge me or tell me what to do, someone who believed in me, who encouraged me to look at some difficult aspects of myself that I don't much like. I examined the very reasons why I wanted to be a principal in the first place. I even began to realize that it wasn't just the kids and the parents and the teachers—it was me, too. There were some things that I had been doing to make life more difficult than it needed to be. Wow! It was an amazing experience.

Consulting With the School Psychologist

Traditionally, school psychologists have focused most of their attention on testing and assessment of children for placement in special programs. However, as they add consulting to their repertoire of services, they offer a wealth of support and information in many areas from individual differences in learning styles and classroom dynamics to multicultural needs and effective behavior management strategies. They offer not only expertise in problem solving with individual students but also prevention services for all students. They can offer programs on a variety of topics such as peer pressure, test anxiety, self-esteem, and loneliness. Furthermore, they will help you identify students at risk and develop programs for them.

When you experience a problem, you will probably feel considerable relief to know that you don't have to "go it alone." In some schools, your first step will be to present the problem for review to an in-school team consisting of several professionals. Then, if the need still persists, the screening committee will make a formal referral to the school psychologist. In other schools, the school psychologist is available to work with staff directly. Both situations allow you to access the expertise of a professional trained specifically to assess children's difficulties and to prescribe programs for remediation.

Consulting With Faculty
at the Local University

Education professors, instructors, and supervisors are often available (some charge consulting fees, of course) to provide help to principals who are experiencing difficulties or who simply have questions on how to handle matters. College faculty can provide consulting, workshops, and teacher training.

One group of teachers in an elementary school was concerned about the high rate of single-parent homes in which their children resided. Because counselors in the district were at a premium, there were few, if any, services offered to address this growing problem. The teachers approached their principal to see if she would support their intent to begin support groups for children experiencing problems adjusting to the separation of their parents. Together they decided to recruit the assistance of faculty at the university, who trained them in the skills and methods of developing such a program. Once the groups began, the counselor education faculty remained available to provide ongoing supervision.

The Principal's Role in Individualized Education Programs

Principals serve as active participants in the development of the Individualized Education Program (IEP) for special education students. Principals know the strengths of each of their team members, the children, and the parents. They are in a unique position to act as an advocate for the student and/or parent. Sometimes, they may even be the only person at an IEP conference who knows everyone in the room.

In general, the principal must be sensitive to the emotions and concerns of the parent(s). When parents are informed that a child may qualify for special help, they typically experience a pattern of reactions: shock, denial, guilt, anger, frustration. Of the people participating in an initial IEP, the principal is the most neutral and objective individual. Therefore, parents may seek out the principal for answers to questions and for emotional support.

At the IEP meeting, assessments will be analyzed and interpreted. The principal can make sure that the professionals (nurse, teacher, psychologist, social worker, counselor) remember to explain their test data and findings in language that is understandable by parents. The principal can watch the parents' nonverbal language during a conference and intercede if results need to be clarified or if educational jargon is overwhelming the parents.

Next, a specific plan will be developed for the forthcoming year. The parents will need a clear description of their child's plan. They will want to know what is expected of them. They will want to know the details of scheduling, times, locations, and transportation, if appropriate. They will want to know what instructional approaches and behavioral strategies will be used. The parents will continue to need the support of the principal, who can help them maintain a positive outlook. The principal can emphasize the strengths of the student and point out where to look for progress in the future.

Principals Are Not Counselors

Although in this chapter, and throughout this book, we have spoken to you about those situations in which you will be functioning like a counselor, you have not had the specialized training (usually the equivalent of 2 years of full-time study) to be counselors. The skills we have presented and the knowledge base we have introduced are only a rudimentary background to help you prepare better for the multiple roles you will play in your profession. Unfortunately, in spite of your best intentions to address all the needs of your school family—psychological as well as academic—you will just not have the time to do the complete job that you would prefer. Your hands will be more than full keeping up with your instructional responsibilities and the support activities that go along with them. Nevertheless, we have shown you a number of ways to integrate counseling methods and skills into your interpersonal style and school environment.

What would you like your staff, students, and parents to say about you 10 years from now? How do you want to be remembered by those with whom you have and will come into contact throughout your career? It would be pleasing if they remembered that you taught them some important things about life, the world, and themselves. But even more fulfilling—imagine that they'll say you really cared about them. You were there for them, really there. They will remember that you were a great listener, someone whom they could trust. You were someone who saw them as individuals. You did not judge them nor did you criticize them (even though you may have been critical of their self-defeating behavior). They will remember that to you, being the principal of their school was not just a job. It was not just something that you did. A principal is who you were. A principal is who you are.

Suggested Activities

1. Answer the following questions in a journal or small-group discussion: Who were the principals who inspired you the most in your life and made you decide to pursue a career in administration? What were they like, and what did they do that made the most difference to you?

2. How would you most like to be remembered as a principal? If a group of your former students and teachers were to meet 20 years from now and talk about you, what would you like them to say?

3. Interview a school counselor, a school psychologist, an administrative colleague, and a professional therapist to find out how they perceive their roles as consultants to parents.

4. Make a list of the situations, problems, and concerns that you feel least prepared to deal with. Start building a resource file of experts in the community with whom you could consult about those situations. Compile a list of resources and support groups that are also available.

5. Based on the topics we have covered in this book, and what you have learned, make a commitment to follow through on three resolutions that you believe are important to your role as a principal. Share them in a group or write them down.

CORWIN PRESS

The Corwin Press logo—a raven striding across an open book—represents the happy union of courage and learning. We are a professional-level publisher of books and journals for K–12 educators, and we are committed to creating and providing resources that embody these qualities. Corwin's motto is "Success for All Learners."